Room For

By
Diane M. Dresback

Room For Another
Copyright © 2018 by Diane M. Dresback

All rights reserved. This book, or parts thereof, may not be reproduced in any form without permission.

This is a work of fiction inspired by true events. All names have been changed. Some characters, places, and incidents are either inspired by true events or are the product of the author's imagination.

Contact Information: www.dianedresback.com

Published by Mindclover Productions LLC
Phoenix, Arizona, USA

GET MY FREE SHORT STORY

Join Diane M. Dresback's Insiders email group and receive a free digital short story prequel to the *Awake As A Stranger* trilogy. By signing up, you will also receive periodic notifications of book releases, free giveaways, and author updates.

This short story prequel offers insight into transformative events that happened to Treaz and to Omani as children; situations that affected who they grew up to be. These two women do not meet until they are adults, but their lives are on target to intertwine in the most peculiar and fascinating manner.

The *Awake As A Stranger* trilogy follows the journey of Treaz and Omani. They reside on two different continents yet each are trapped in deplorable realities—Treaz living within other people's bodies and Omani being held captive on her uncle's compound.

Both long to regain control over their lives, escape their merciless captors, and expose the haunting truths facing them and the world. Can they find freedom together?

Get YOUR Free digital short story by visiting
www.dianedresback.com

BOOKS BY DIANE M. DRESBACK

TRILOGY

Awake As A Stranger trilogy
Awakening (Book 1)
Rebellion (Book 2)
Altercation (Book 3)

STAND ALONES

Postponement

Reminisce

Promise of Protection

Room For Another:
A Courageous Adoption Story Based on True Events

NONFICTION

From Us For You: Inspiring Stories of Healing, Growth and Transformation

Your Action, Your Success: Motivating Yourself To Get Things Done

DEDICATION

To all my parents for their varied personalities and willingness to love me. I have been loved!

ACKNOWLEDGEMENTS

Trenton Greyoak and Devon Dresback for always supporting my creative projects.

Rick Silber for forever believing in my story-telling aspirations.

Terri Cox for all you endured for me.

Deanna and Trenton Greyoak for cover design.

Teresa Young for delineating discrepancies in my characters and my story.

The North Texas Writers MeetUp group for invaluable feedback during the writing process.

Charles and Mildred Gerg for picking me up out of the ditch.

AUTHOR'S NOTE

Room For Another is written as a novel, yet is based mostly on true events. I thought long and hard about how best to present this story as shared with me. Even though I've done my best to stay truthful, this book is not meant to relay hard facts. Everyone remembers things in their own ways. I've had to imagine many conversations and interactions (hence not a memoir, but rather a novel). For those who know the characters in real life, please allow me the liberty of a writer to not be factual in all areas while remaining truthful to the mandate given to me by the main character. The real names of all involved have been changed. Also, there are some completely fictional characters.

Above all, I want readers to enjoy the story, appreciating the tender, heart-breaking, and fun-loving moments.

CHAPTER 1
(2006)

A blaring alarm echoed loudly against the high ceilings of the workshop causing Theresa to jump and jab her index finger with a quilting needle.

"Ouch," exclaimed Theresa turning off the annoying racket and slipping her wounded finger in her mouth. The clock read 2:30 p.m., indicating it was time to make good on her favor promised to Miss Stacy Hershey, a new high school teacher that Theresa had befriended a year earlier.

"I need your help," Stacy had said. "You know Darcy Noble and Liz Valdez?"

"Purchased many Girl Scout cookies from them over the years. Still have an unopened box of Thin Mints in the back of my pantry…somewhere," said Theresa. "What's the problem?"

"I had them for creative writing last year. Both smart, excellent writers. Easily "A" students. But this semester in my journalism class, they're only doing "C" work."

Despite being long since retired from teaching the elementary grades, Theresa still loved children of any age, even the ones that came with challenges—which were most of them. The enthusiasm and curiosity of youth energized her as opposed to the assumptions and know-it-all attitude of adults, herself now included.

"Why?" asked Theresa.

"I'll give you one guess."

Theresa smiled. "Boys."

"Yes. And they're bored as can be and turning in mediocre work. Just the bare minimum to squeak by."

Theresa often helped her grandchildren with homework as well as needy young neighbors, always encouraging them to put their studies first and stay in school—usually an outdated mantra kids heard daily from most of their parents, but not all.

"They've partnered up on an interview assignment that's due in a couple weeks, but I've seen no progress from either of them. I want them to be inspired. Would you consider being their interviewee? Do you have some good stories to share with them?"

Theresa cocked her head. "Why, yes I do. I'd be happy to help."

So, today was the day.

She groaned at the crimson smear across the fabric of her latest project—a pink and white quilt for a newborns' crib. While dabbing the stain with hydrogen peroxide, her eyes grew misty at the thought of a first-born, precious little girl making her way into the world to join her new family. Theresa adored babies.

The deadline for the handmade quilt loomed but it could be pushed back—again. She reasoned that exceptional craft took time and her meticulous work with material, scissors, and a needle, remained in high demand, not only with the tourists traveling through the small northern California town but also by friends of friends who came to know her unique quilting patterns and beautiful color ensembles—minus the blood.

Theresa fluffed her short silver hair, gathered her purse, and walked outside into the warm air. For the past month, when not fighting to stay up with quilting orders, Theresa and her daughter, Mary, stayed busy canning from the harvest of their gardens—their shelves filling with jars of plum jelly, dill pickle spears, and green tomato relish. There was still much to finish, but helping Stacy and the girls, sounded important.

Theresa fished in her bag locating a half-finished pack of Benson and Hedges Menthol Lights. Better do it now. She didn't want to promote that specific vice to the girls. Yet, by this time they likely could tell by the deepening lines on her face. None of the expensive facial creams tried over the years worked to erase the ever-growing evidence. The habit began at twenty-three following one of the most stressful periods in her life. Theresa imagined that story would be coming out in the interview, along with many others she hadn't thought about in a while. After the strike of a match, she inhaled the calm. She'd work on stopping another day.

Not only did Theresa smoke, so did her beloved nine-year-old Plymouth Breeze gray four-door sedan. On the way to her meeting, it was hard to ignore the giveaway trail of bluish haze visible in the rear-view mirror. She chuckled. Maybe someday they'd quit together.

The small town coffee shop was cheery in its decor. Even though it was 2006, the red and white checkered curtains and glassed lithographs of Elvis Presley and James Dean attempted to offer a more nostalgic feel. Theresa sat savoring a cup of fancy java with just the perfect amount of froth floating on top—the foam being a delicacy one of the young employees had introduced her to a few months back.

3

If not for her enjoying a moment of stillness, the tardiness of the students might have irritated her—a pet-peeve held over from her teaching days.

She gazed at the modern-day jukebox intended to appear as if it came right out of a fifties malt shop with its yellow and red colors and numbered buttons. *Wake Up Little Susie* by the Everly Brothers played. Theresa allowed her eyes to close recalling how she struggled to dance to that song when she was in college. Both of her left feet tromping on her partner's feet. And, that boy…

A merry jingle announced the entrance of new customers, and Theresa opened her eyes, saw the girls, and waved them over. They rushed to the booth and clambered in plopping over-stuffed backpacks on the table.

"We're so sorry, Ms. Clavin," said Darcy. "Liz just got her license and she drives like a snail."

"Hey," responded Liz as she poked her friend with her elbow.

Theresa remembered being well in her twenties before obtaining a license to drive. "I'm glad you got here safely." She looked at Darcy with her neat blonde ponytail and smartly applied makeup. "How's your grandmother doing after her surgery?"

Darcy pulled a crinkled paper and pen from her backpack. "She's getting better."

Theresa nodded and addressed Liz. "And your mother? I see she's expecting again."

Liz sighed and scratched her scalp of multi-colored hair worn in a pixie cut. Thick eyeliner curled up slightly at the edges of her eyes, a small spec of a jewel donned the left side of her nose. "She's at that throw-up stage."

Theresa chuckled. "Ah, remember it well."

"Thanks for agreeing to do this, Ms. Clavin," Liz said. "The paper's for our journalism class. We got to interview an old person about—"

"Liz," exclaimed Darcy, horrified.

Liz covered her mouth. "That was way rude. Sorry."

"I'm very familiar with the perception teens hold for the concept of age," Theresa said. "A more appropriate description might be, an elderly person, which probably means anyone over thirty to you two."

Darcy grimaced. "Sorry."

Theresa gave a dismissive wave of her hand, the comment not really bothering her. "What does Miss Hershey classify as old?"

The girls both shrugged.

"Over fifty?" Liz said, raising her voice in question.

This brought a smile to Theresa's face. "Is she looking for anything in particular?"

"Um. Just a few significant stories from your growing up," said Darcy.

"Ha. I'm still growing up."

Two boys, mature in stature and sprouting whiskers, passed by the table, one winking at Liz. She smiled shyly in return.

Theresa noticed the exchange. "You like him, Liz?"

Darcy nodded enthusiastically. "Oh yeah, she does. He's like the hottest guy in school."

Theresa arched her eyebrows. She now was on a mission to educate these girls a little bit about boys. "How long does this paper need to be?"

"As long as we want," answered Liz. "We've got until 4:30, then I gotta go pick up my sister. But, that should be enough time."

Theresa didn't try to stifle her snicker. "You want to know about my life in two hours...no wait," she consulted her watch. "Ninety-five minutes now?"

The girls gave blank expressions.

"How about this. I was born during a wildfire, my parents swapped spouses, I moved more times than I can count, I went to college, lived with a man thirty-five years my senior, gave a baby up for adoption, taught school, wrote for a newspaper, had two more children but raised many more. How's that?" She held a straight-face waiting for a response.

They stared back at her.

"Um," said Liz.

Theresa knew she had them hooked, softened her sarcasm, and leaned forward. "Tell you what. I won't burden you with all the detailed ins-and-outs of my life, and if after today you think you have enough to write an A-worthy paper, then fine. But if not, I'll agree to meet with you twice more this week and share a few rather interesting things. I'm going out of town next Monday."

The students glanced at each other.

"And, free coffee and dessert, my treat," Theresa added.

Darcy and Liz nodded together.

"Alright then. Why don't you both get something up front and we'll get started." They took the twenty dollar bill Theresa slid across the table and went to peruse the menu.

"Do you want something to eat, Ms. Clavin?" called out Darcy from the counter.

"No, thanks," said Theresa, honestly preferring a cigarette. Having not shared some of these experiences for a long time, she expected they would stir up some emotions, but it would be good for her to revisit them with young, impressionable teenagers.

Soon, her interviewers were back. Darcy carrying a steaming mug with a chocolate stir sticking out, and a giant chocolate chip cookie with one bite already taken. Liz with black coffee and a slice of crumbly apple pie. The girls settled in.

Darcy prepared to make notes on her paper. "Okay. We gotta find out a couple things first. Your full name and birthdate."

"Theresa Susan Clavin. June twenty-seventh, 1936. Yes, that makes me seventy this year. I qualify as old." She laughed.

Darcy handed the paper to Theresa. "And you gotta sign this saying it's okay for us to write about you."

Theresa scanned the paper, scribbled her signature, and returned it.

After Darcy tucked the permission slip back into her backpack, she and Liz opened their laptops and waited for Theresa to begin.

"There's so much to tell, but I'll start with a few stories from my early years." Theresa gave a long exhale. "My father was a ranger in southern California. The day I was born, he was called off the fire lines to rush my mother fifty miles away to a hospital in San Diego. After I was delivered, by cesarean section, my mother was told she couldn't have any more children due to being too small and having a blood issue."

Darcy and Liz made notes on their computers in between bites of dessert and sips of coffee.

"Forestry rangers and their families were transferred quite often all around California. That meant always needing to make new friends. The forestry compounds were usually out of town, so there weren't many other children around." Theresa tilted her head. "And then World War II started."

CHAPTER 2
(1942 - 1943)

The bus dropped six-year-old Theresa off at a forestry compound in northern California. She skipped home to inform her most favorite person in the whole world all about the full day at school. She found her mother busy at the sewing machine and kissed her on the cheek.

"Hi, Momma."

"Hello, honey." But Ann neither looked up nor embraced her daughter like usual. Theresa watched the needle rhythmically go in and out, in and out, of long thick strips of black material. She instantly recognized her mother's task because not long after moving into that little house, Theresa had learned how to cut floral patterned fabric pieces in the same manner.

Ann zig-zagged at the end of the hem and snipped the thread.

Theresa frowned. Hems were supposed to be hand-stitched.

"Why do we need those ugly curtains?" Theresa asked. "I like our pretty flower ones."

Her mother stood and shook out the stiff, drab new window coverings. "So no one can see our lights shining at night."

"But, I like seeing the stars."

Ann motioned her daughter for assistance. "Yes, but we must use these for now. Here. Help me." The two of them carried the heavy drapes to the first window and Theresa held the step-stool as her mother began hanging them.

Her father came in and spoke sternly. "Theresa, you must not open the curtains even a little. Do you hear me?"

Theresa nodded, not fully understanding, but sensing that she shouldn't protest.

Every night her mother slid the drapery shut and left them that way until the morning light.

One night not long after the curtains were drawn and everyone slept, sirens began to blare. Theresa bounded into her parents' room and straight into the arms of her mother, burying her face in Ann's soft robe. These were not forest fire warnings, but something different. Gunfire boomed in the distance down by the coastline.

Harold pulled on his shirt, then his black jacket.

Theresa watched him. "Where are you going, Daddy?"

Ann answered for her husband. "Daddy's going to check to be sure everyone else's drapes are closed up tight. We don't want bad people in the airplanes to know we're here."

"But—" began Theresa. She stopped when Harold gave his wife a glance, then strode out.

Still clinging to her waist, Theresa looked up to her mother. "We closed ours, right?"

Ann nodded and motioned her daughter to the bed. They climbed in together. Theresa eventually fell back to sleep curled tightly into Momma.

The next morning, Theresa carried her dirty breakfast dishes to the sink where her mother stood gazing out the window. Her father entered through the back door, looking tired.

Ann put down her dish towel. "Harold, what happened?"

"Sub came too close to shore," he mumbled before disappearing into the bathroom.

From then on the town sirens wailed quite frequently. Each time, Ann comforted Theresa's fears as Harold walked the neighborhood checking for compliance of the government blackout regulation.

Although she hated the sirens, Theresa did grow accustomed to the daily consequences of war. Momma received coupons and food ration books with special stamps with which to purchase all the items being rationed—sugar, meat, gasoline, shoes, chocolate, and even the hose Ann wore. Theresa helped her mother collect the grease from their cooking and turned it into the butcher at the store. She regularly joined with others in putting everything normally tossed in the trash into large cans set up at the end of the streets. Her teacher at school said that some of the contents collected were manufactured into bullets to help fight the war. Theresa wanted to do her part.

Several weeks later, Theresa awoke in one of her fondest places—her maternal grandparents' home. Grandma cooked on a giant wooden stove making horribly sticky oatmeal for breakfast while Grandpa sat on the porch drinking coffee. Most of the afternoon, he half-dozed as his granddaughter amused herself by counting the fruit and playing amongst the mature avocado trees that filled the acreage behind the house.

Theresa fed and chased the chickens naming each after the children in her class at school. She pointed and called out, "Barbara, Veronica, Bobbie, Jessica…"

"Hey Miss T, let's go," shouted Grandpa at dusk. She turned, and he stood holding a bucket and a long-handled spear with a three-pronged end. Theresa grinned knowing the menu for dinner that night and ran to fetch the flashlight. They walked down to the creek together talking about school, the war, her friends, and whatever other subjects arose on the way to their destination—a pond half-a-mile away. Theresa didn't know what she liked better, the time spent with her grandfather or the thrill of frogging.

Once at the swampy water, Grandpa was all business. She shined the bright light until they spotted eyes reflecting back. He determined they were the correct type of eyes, and quickly pierced the creature using the long-handled spear. The first spoils for the night went into the bucket and they continued the hunt. When they got back, they handed the bucket over to Grandma. Although Theresa disliked the gruesome job of cutting off the frogs legs, she did giggle as they jumped in the fry pan.

Suddenly, air-raid sirens began to wail and Theresa's heart immediately pounded as it always did at the eerie warning. Her mother quickly walked to the window and drew the blackout curtains as a fleet of airplanes roared overhead.

Grandma placed her hand atop Theresa's head. "Say a prayer that God keeps those boys safe."

Theresa obediently clasped her hands, bowed her head, and squeezed her eyes shut to pray for those brave men.

The next afternoon, her grandmother insisted that no one ever went home with empty bellies, and directed her husband outside for the main course. Theresa followed him and cringed at his task. He reached down, caught one of the unsuspecting chickens by the neck, swung it above his head, and then held it out to Theresa. She swallowed back the lump in her throat and brought the dead bird into Grandma who taught Theresa how to de-feather and prepare it for cooking.

As the aroma of baking poultry filled the kitchen, Theresa peeled endless potatoes. Grandma generously used her rationed milk and butter to make the mashed potatoes extra creamy.

A few hours later they all sat down in front of a savory, golden delight. When Grandpa cut into the tender chicken, he winked at Theresa. "Jessica provided for us, today."

Theresa couldn't help but smile remembering how she had named one of the chicken's Jessica.

When they bid farewell, Grandpa handed Theresa a small Bible. "This is for you."

Her mouth fell open. "My first one." She opened the brown leather cover, saw the inscription with her name, and hugged him. "I love it. Thank you, Grandpa."

After a move to another forestry town, Theresa noticed her parents fighting more often, their arguments loud and vicious. She hated when they fought and it always made her tummy hurt. But, she didn't know what to do. After her seventh birthday, she stood by the kitchen door listening to her mother and father scream at each other.

"Of all women, Harold. You know she hates children," yelled Ann.

Theresa peeked around the corner wondering who Momma was talking about.

"Do you even love me?" her mother asked her father.

Theresa's chest clenched. Her father's silence—more heart-wrenching than any words. She thought if she walked in, perhaps they would stop arguing, so she entered the room. For a handful of minutes, the quarrel ceased and there was silence, yet a heaviness remained in the air. Theresa sat quietly, her gaze alternating between her parents. Her scowling father would not meet her eye. Her mother's face red and eyes watery. Ann's hands shook while serving up three plates of spaghetti. Afraid to say anything to either of them, Theresa focused on the mound piled on her plate.

For a while, Ann stared at her food as well, and Theresa thought perhaps her mother wasn't hungry. Then unexpectedly, Ann lifted her full plate and heaved it across the table at her husband. Theresa began to laugh at the sight—dangling pasta, red sauce, and broken meatballs dripping from Harold's shirt onto the floor—but she stopped when she saw Ann begin to cry.

Not knowing how to react, Theresa bolted from the kitchen to her bedroom, slamming the door. The yelling erupted once again with increased fury as the girl pulled the pillow around her ears, attempting to drown out the noise. "Please God, make them stop."

Not long after that, Ann and Harold separated, then divorced. Theresa was heartbroken at the breakup of her family. Yet at last her parents' quarreling stopped. She discovered she rather enjoyed having her mother all to herself even though this meant she and her mother had to move again! They lived with her grandparents for a short time, then moved in with Ann's sister, Aunt Mable, and Theresa's three cousins. Uncle Brad was away fighting in Germany.

Theresa liked the visits from her father, but they always ended up with a squabble between Ann and Harold when he brought her home. He began to come less and less.

After one stretch of six months, Harold appeared. "Theresa, we're going to a nice hotel in the city. I'm treating you to a special lunch."

Theresa loved that he was acting extra affectionate towards her, and she gobbled it up. All the way she chatted happily about her friends and her new teacher at school. She told him how after her tonsils were removed, Momma had rewarded her with a new cocker-spaniel puppy named Vicky.

When Harold and Theresa reached the hotel, she marveled at the perfect planters brimming with striking red, yellow, and purple blossoms, and curving brick-paved pathways meandering through the gardens appealing to the eight-year-old's sense of exploration.

Her father took her hand. "Come on. I've got a surprise for you."

It felt good to hold his hand again—she had missed him. He led her into the grandiose lobby decorated with gold-framed paintings and over-sized mirrors.

They approached an open elevator where a young woman dressed in a neat blue skirt and jacket stood waiting. She smiled at Theresa. "Hello there, young lady."

Theresa returned the greeting. "Hello."

"Third floor," said Harold.

"Yes Sir."

As the car glided quietly to the third floor, Theresa couldn't help but stare from the corner of her eye at the elevator operator's perfected make-up, hair, and posture. She wondered if when she grew up she might look like this lady, although she couldn't imagine being cooped up in an elevator all day no matter how glamorous it looked inside. That wasn't for her. When they exited, Theresa thanked the woman and stood straighter in her own dress, one Momma had sewed.

They walked down the bold red and green carpet past numbered guest room doors with brass knockers. Theresa loved gifts and the anticipation of receiving her surprise made her stomach flutter with butterflies. At the last door, Harold looked down at his daughter. "You ready?" She nodded, an eager smile across her face.

He opened the door and standing there was Dorothy.

Theresa's smile vanished and shoulders slumped. She had history with Dorothy and her ex-husband, Carl, as they'd been friends of her parents. Harold and Carl met while working for the forestry service and soon Theresa found the couple socializing at her house on many occasions. She helped Ann make hors d'oeuvres for them to eat while they played cards and drank cocktails. Carl, a big burly man with a Texas drawl, had always been friendly. However, Dorothy never spoke much to Theresa. After a few evenings together, Theresa picked up on Ann's coolness toward Dorothy. Theresa agreed. Dorothy wasn't real nice. She wore a perpetual frown—the exact one she wore on her face standing in front of Theresa now.

"Dorothy and I are married," her father announced with resolution.

Seeing Dorothy, coupled with the awful revelation that she was to be her stepmother, seemed incomprehensible to Theresa. It couldn't be true.

"What do you say?" Harold said, embarrassed by his daughters' impolite silence.

Furious, she crossed her arms and turned her back on them both. She wanted nothing to do with that woman.

Harold pushed the door closed. An awkward twenty minutes followed as her father unsuccessfully tried anger, sweet-talking, bribery, and reasoning, but Theresa responded to none of it. All the while, Dorothy said nothing to the angry little girl.

Trying a new tactic, Harold glanced at his watch and said, "Let's go to lunch. We have reservations at the fancy restaurant downstairs." He tried to take his daughter's hand but she refused and walked out of the room with arms still folded across her chest.

Theresa did not speak or eat. She wanted to go home. Harold put a small wrapped package on the table in front of her, but she ignored the shiny paper and delicate bow. He's trying to trick her. Theresa picked up the box and threw it back at her father, just as her mother had thrown her plate of spaghetti. He deserved it. Life with her father would not ever be the same with such a horrible woman. How could he have done this to her? Dorothy would never be her mother!

She held back her tears and said curtly, "I'll be outside." Theresa stormed out of the restaurant ignoring the nearby patrons whispering about the spoiled little girl's inappropriate behavior.

As soon as Harold arrived back at Ann's house, Theresa dashed in blurting out the news. The biggest, most terrible battle ensued between her parents.

CHAPTER 3
(2006)

"That fight kept my father away for three years," said Theresa as she stopped for a drink of coffee.

"He never called or nothing?" asked Darcy.

"Anything," Theresa said as she shook her head. "Not that I knew of."

"What happened to your mom?" said Liz.

"One year later, she began taking me up to the drug store pay phone and making me wait in the car. Luckily, I loved to read because we were there a lot. No matter how hard I strained, I couldn't hear my mother's conversation. But, I knew whoever she was talking to, they were making her smile which made me happy."

Liz opened her eyes wide. "Was it a guy?"

"I kept prodding her to tell me and finally she admitted that she'd been talking to Carl, Dorothy's ex-husband."

"What?" exclaimed Liz.

"No way," said Darcy. "Dorothy, your dad's wife?"

Theresa put up her hands. "I know. My parents swapped partners."

"That's, like, weird," concluded Darcy. "But, you liked him, right?"

"I loved Carl. He had a kind way about him and he cared about me. He had these enormous arms and hugged me all the time. It was good to see him treating my mother so well. They eventually married, and I was excited to have Carl as my stepfather. The only bad thing was he lived up here in northern California, over in Quincy, and we were living in southern California. So my mother, me and Vicky the dog, all moved to live in his home."

Darcy stopped typing. "Did Dorothy and him have kids?"

"They had a seventeen-year-old daughter. At first, I thought it might be fun to have an older sister, but she didn't like us even before we got there, so she stayed as far away as possible."

"Why didn't she live with her mom?" Liz asked.

Theresa raised her eyebrows. "I asked my mother the same question. Apparently, the judge decided that because Dorothy had cheated on her husband with my father, her daughter could not stay with her."

Darcy frowned. "Wait. What?"

"Definitely old-fashioned now. But, this was in the 1940s." Theresa leaned closer. "I certainly would hate to live with Dorothy."

"No doubt," said Liz.

CHAPTER 4
(1945 - 1946)

Theresa was thrilled when the war finally ended in 1945. No more air-raids and now she could savor the taste of chocolate bars, again. She loved spending time with her mother, planting their garden and learning how to can the fruit they had grown. That year, they spent hours walking in the forest hunting for the best Christmas tree and the ideal yule log to burn on Christmas Eve. Everything felt perfect.

At age nine, Theresa met Julianna. A tall, slender girl with a freckly face and long red hair. Her father was a prospector whose job entailed hiking through the High Sierra Mountains in California, in search of gold. Theresa was thrilled when Julianna's father allowed the girls to go with him. They'd traipse way back in the hills, where no one had been in years, going from sunrise to sunset. He taught them how to pan for gold in the chilly streams.

On weekends Theresa and Julianna panned until they had enough 'color,' then would take their findings to the local jeweler. He would give them just enough money to gain access to another favorite past-time—the Saturday afternoon matinee.

With the sides being all logs, the theatre looked like a cabin. The girls happily handed over their nickels to watch a cartoon, the latest episode of *Roy Rogers* or *Superman*, plus a movie, all the while munching on salt and butter-drenched popcorn. Their routine included a stop by the drug store on the way home to eat homemade peach ice cream.

Carl had quit his forestry job and purchased a car dealership on the main street in town. One hot summer night, when everything felt sticky, Ann and Theresa drove to pick Carl up from work. They entered the building and found him talking to a customer. The ancient man had a weathered unshaven face and hunched back. Theresa covered her nose because of his sharp, unbathed odor. He was admiring an expensive Cadillac glistening on the showroom floor.

Theresa's stepfather left the man and came over to Ann and Theresa. He tilted his head at his unconventional customer, and whispered, rather sarcastically. "I'll be done with this guy soon. Why don't you wait across the street in the hotel lobby?"

"Alright," said Ann.

Theresa enjoyed going to the hotel because the clerk behind the counter always gave her a cookie. But long after the treat was eaten, and at least an hour had passed, they returned to the dealership to find out what was taking so long.

They found Carl seated across from the old man. Rusty coffee cans covered the desk and the floor, all brimming with gold and coins. Theresa's eyes grew. She had never seen so much gold in all her life. Carl glanced up at them and shrugged. Soon the jeweler arrived with his scales. All the gold was weighed and money counted until there was enough to pay for the car.

After the beaming new owner loaded the remaining coffee cans into the back seat of his brand-new Cadillac, he drove off leaving behind the oldest and most beat-up pickup truck Theresa had ever seen. She giggled when later that night, Carl paid for their pricey restaurant meal using gold dust.

Theresa was thankful that the next move for their family allowed them to stay in the same area, only higher up the mountain. At first her mother was angry with Carl for buying such a wreck of a house. The tiny log home, built in the 1880s, was in dire need of fixing and seemed barely inhabitable. Yet, Theresa didn't mind. She imagined endless new places to explore as the structure was located next to a bright meadow with hummingbirds lighting on the wildflower blossoms, and a small bubbling creek with massive pines and cedar trees reaching higher than Theresa dared to climb.

Over time, her family worked together to repair and expand the home. Although not large, it seemed cozy and filled with pride from all their efforts.

One very clear summer night, Ann and Theresa took a blanket and pillows out on the front lawn. They lay there gazing up to the twinkling stars. Vicky, the cocker spaniel, and two kittens curled up close by.

"Look you can see nearly all the way up to heaven," Ann said warmly. Suddenly, a shooting star streaked across the sky.

"Ooooh," exclaimed Theresa, pointing. "Did you see it?"

Her mother nodded. "Yes. Do you know what that means?"

"No. What?"

"Someone has just gone to heaven and you should pray for them."

Theresa thought for a moment. "What do I say?"

Her mother folded her hands together and closed her eyes. "Bless them Lord and welcome them home."

Theresa joined her hands and squeezed her eyes shut while repeating the prayer. They watched for more falling stars until bedtime.

Theresa walked to meet Julianna for their usual Saturday afternoon movie plans. The weather was brutally hot, so Theresa yanked the bands from her hair and placed her head underneath the hose behind the drugstore. The coolness of the water trickling down her back offered sweet relief from the heat. She tied the wet mess up into a big knot on top of her head. Theresa disliked the pigtails that her mother always insisted on to keep her hair from tangling. They were just too inviting for playful or irritating people to tug on. The day before, the boy sitting behind her in class stuck the ends into the inkwell on his desk.

Then, Theresa caught the faint whiff of smoke and the mill whistles blew. All too familiar with what that meant, fear struck and she took off running.

CHAPTER 5
(1946)

As she ran, Theresa watched thin tendrils of smoke swirl and sway up into the blue sky. The whistles shrilled out long and short tones. Theresa knew they were to inform the volunteer crews of the fire location. When she arrived home, she flew into the arms of her mother who stood outside watching. Together they witnessed the flames spread over the mountaintop of their town, the dragon of fire expanding in all directions, consuming everything in its path.

In addition to the mill whistles, sirens began to blare indicating immediate evacuation. Theresa's eyes filled with tears not wanting to leave their home she'd grown to love. Would everything burn up? She feared fire.

Theresa heard neighborhood parents calling for their children and pets. Young children cried as the panic to get out settled into the community.

"Theresa," said Ann. "Hose down the cabin and the neighbors' houses."

Theresa ran to the hose by the side of their house, picked it up, and began doing as she was told. She covered her nose as the air rapidly filled with smoke. She hated fire.

After a few minutes, Ann walked up to Theresa, took a firm hold of her shoulders, and looked straight in her eyes. "Today will be scary for you, but you are to grow up even more. You will listen and obey every word I say. Do you understand?"

Unable to speak, she nodded, her eyes wide, heart pounding. She knew they'd be staying and not evacuating with everyone else. There was no time for crying, no time. She despised fire so much!

Theresa followed her mother into the house.

"Make as many peanut butter sandwiches as you can," Ann directed, and Theresa went to work.

As she smeared peanut butter sloppily onto slices of bread, she watched her mother snatch the first aid kit from the kitchen cupboard and take all the sheets from their closet. Using water from the bathtub, Ann filled the five-gallon cans from their porch. From the kitchen window, Theresa saw her load everything into the trunk of the car. With no more bread, Theresa stuffed all the sandwiches into paper bags and carried them to the car, placing them on the back seat. They both jumped in and drove toward the forestry station.

The town was eerily deserted—the log theatre, the drug store, the post office. Most people had left their homes and businesses and were in their vehicles moving out of town traveling in both lanes. Theresa saw the baker's wife comforting a lost little boy. His face tear-stained as he held tightly to a white cat. Theresa hoped they'd find his momma.

They passed by the Cadillac dealership, which was void of any people. Theresa realized she'd forgotten to ask earlier. "Where's Carl?"

"Helping fill the engines," said her mother. That made sense as he previously worked for the forestry service. Theresa was relieved he wasn't on the fire line.

Once at the station, they saw men sitting on the ground or on picnic benches. Theresa had met many of them. Some had given her butterscotch candies or tugged on her pigtails in the past, but not that day. The smoke made their faces black and eyes red.

"Go into the kitchen and help," said Ann. Theresa did so without question and stayed busy alongside the firefighters' wives making more sandwiches than she had ever made in her life. She delivered them to the weary firefighters along with cups of cold water and bottles of soda. Some thanked her, others just accepted without speaking. Once finished, Theresa watched the men return into a strange orange cast of smoke that blotted out the sun. They were so brave.

When it got dark, the red lit up the skyline. For just a moment, Theresa thought about how beautiful it looked but guilt quickly struck her for even thinking something so destructive could be beautiful.

Theresa hadn't seen her mother in hours and went to search for her. She entered the barracks and struggled to comprehend the sight. Ann and the local doctor treated the injured men who lay on cots and on the floor. The air smelled like a mixture of stale smoke and burned flesh. Theresa immediately began to gag but had no opportunity to leave.

"Theresa!" Ann called out. "Come help me."

She ran over.

"Tear that sheet into strips," instructed Ann.

Theresa saw her mother's face beaded with sweat, and blood smeared across the front of her dress. She wanted to reach out and hug her, but she did as instructed and held out each of the make-shift bandages. The man screamed in agony as his horrible wounds were dressed. Theresa tried not to react. Then they moved on to the next man. And the next. She was too focused to cry as they helped with terrible burns, deep splinters, chain-saw cuts, red eyes unable to see. They toiled together for what seemed like hours to Theresa until finally, her mother took Theresa out for a break.

In the office, Ann poured herself some coffee and gave Theresa a soda. For a while they listened to the radio. The men called in about the status of the blaze and the dispatcher provided further information and assignments.

Beyond exhausted, Theresa lay down in the corner next to a file cabinet, slipped off dirty shoes from her aching feet, and closed her eyes. It felt so good to stop and rest.

She awoke to her mother yelling, and Theresa sat up. Other firefighters came into the dispatch room. One of them put his arm around Ann's shoulder.

Everything grew quiet.

During the radio conversation back and forth, Theresa's heart weighed heavy in her chest. She realized that a fire truck was surrounded by flames and the firefighters could not escape.

One at a time, the four men's voices crackled across the airwaves. They shared words of regret, encouragement to be strong, but mostly expressions of immense love and gratitude for wives, children, parents, and siblings.

The dispatcher frantically wrote down each final message to their families.

Then the radio went dead.

All was silent except for Ann's sobbing.

Theresa curled back up. She squeezed her eyes tight, hoping to evade the anguish of tragedy by falling back to sleep.

For three more days, the fire destroyed all the forest around the town, taking along many homes, and displacing entire families. Eventually, the Army brought in fresh crews and supplies, and Theresa, Ann, and Carl returned home.

Thankful that their house remained untouched by the flames, Theresa snuggled and played with Vicky all afternoon. That night, Ann appeared in Theresa's room just as she always did, and they said their prayers.

Her mother pulled the blanket up to her daughter's chin and kissed her on the forehead. "I'm very proud of you," she said.

Theresa smiled. She loved that her Momma was proud. Ann switched off the light and closed the door. As Theresa fell asleep, she realized her mother had been correct. She had grown up a little more over those three days.

In the fall of fifth grade, Ann made an announcement to her daughter—one that would affect Theresa's life in a most unexpected way.

CHAPTER 6
(1946 - 1947)

Ann revealed that Theresa was to have a new baby brother or sister. Theresa jumped up and down like a rabbit, making her mother laugh at her daughter's enthusiasm.

"Thank you, Momma, thank you," she said throwing her arms around her mother and squeezing her tightly. She dashed out of the house shouting, "I gotta tell Julianna."

For five months, all proceeded smoothly. Theresa constantly touched her mother's belly hoping to feel the baby move. She enjoyed talking about possible names, and what newborn clothes her mother could sew.

Then Ann grew very ill and did not get better. When Grandma showed up to handle the household duties, Theresa sensed the seriousness of things. Carl took his wife to the doctor and when they arrived home, he carried her to bed.

Theresa watched, sick with worry. "Momma, are you going to be alright?"

"Let your mother rest, now," said Carl as he ushered the girl out of the room and closed the door.

She followed him to the family room. "What's wrong? Is the baby okay?"

Carl sat down next to Theresa. "The doctor said your mother must remain in bed for the rest of her pregnancy or the baby will die."

The baby might die? It mustn't die! Theresa decided she would help as much as she could.

For the next four months, as Ann stayed in bed, Theresa and Julianna spent hours with her reading, making up stories, playing cards, and studying words from the dictionary. Most of the time, Vicky lay curled up on the foot of the bed raising her eyebrows occasionally at the laughter and activity. Theresa knew whenever her mother became weary because she'd send the girls off to play and do their childhood merrymaking.

Late one afternoon, Theresa and Julianna sat together in a large rocking chair by the fireplace. They sipped hot chocolate and ate peanut butter cookies that Grandma had baked. Vicky licked up every wayward crumb. The young girls spoke of plans for the next day—where they could walk to find new places to explore. Their scheming ceased when Ann shuffled in the room, her robe tied around her full-term belly. Carl escorted her to the couch.

"Momma, why are you out of bed?"

"Come here, Theresa," beckoned Ann, patting the cushion next to her. Theresa came close fearful that perhaps she had done something wrong.

Ann took hold of her daughter's hand and began to speak, but choked up. She took a deep breath and started again. "I may not be coming home to you."

Theresa just stared at her mother. She didn't understand.

"You have been such a joy in my life. You will always be…be in my heart. All you have to do is talk to me and you'll know I'm right there with you." Ann touched Theresa's chest.

What did she mean? "But..." The lump in Theresa's throat prevented her from saying more.

Salty water began to well in all their eyes. Carl placed his hand on his wife's shoulder. She glanced up at him, then back to her daughter. She stroked Theresa's face and they hugged.

Theresa did not want to let go. "Momma?"

"Be sure to pick the first strawberries and with each one you eat, think of me," said Ann before kissing Theresa.

Carl helped his wife stand, scooped her up in his arms, and headed out the front door.

"Momma?" Theresa squeaked, her eyes blurry with tears, her body heavy. "I don't understand."

"Don't forget to sing to me," Ann said, looking back. "You have such a pretty voice. Remember...I love you."

Carl disappeared with Ann as Grandma shut the door.

Theresa sunk to the floor, numbness overtaking her body. "I love you too, Momma."

Despite Theresa's protests, her grandmother insisted she spend the night with Julianna. The eleven-year-old girls snuggled together in the tiny bed. Theresa listened to her friend's rhythmic breathing and wondered what her mother had meant by her words. Her mother always had come home. Always.

Early the next morning, she crawled from the warmth of the down comforter to gaze out the window. A shooting star streaked across the dark sky and she gasped. Quickly folding her hands and closing her eyes, she whispered, "Bless them Lord and welcome them home." Then she hesitated before adding an extra request. "Please God, make it the baby that died, not Momma."

That morning, Julianna's father invited the girls to go panning for gold, one of Theresa's favorite things to do, yet she declined. She wanted to be ready to go when Carl came to take her home and back to her mother. Late in the afternoon, Carl walked up the drive to Julianna's house, his head hanging. With a sudden pain in her stomach, Theresa immediately knew. Her mother's star had fallen. Momma had gone home to be with God. She flung open the front door and rushed past Carl.

"Theresa!"

She did not stop but ran up the mountain path to a cliff she and Julianna often tossed rocks over, watching them bounce off the canyon walls far below.

"I hate you," Theresa screamed up at the blue sky, her body trembling with anger. "How could you do this? Send her back. Send my Momma back. I don't want that baby. I want my Momma."

Theresa stepped closer to the jagged edge. If God wouldn't bring Momma back, she'd just go and be with her in heaven. Surely God would let her in, wouldn't he? God loved little girls, didn't he?

Before she could reason anymore, Carl came up from behind and scooped her up in his big arms, as he had done so often with her mother.

Through his sobs, he confirmed her nightmare. "Your mother died last night right after your baby brother was born."

Theresa could not cry—her anger paralyzing.

He took her back down to his truck and they drove home.

There was a lot of silence in their cabin that night. Grandma fixed dinner, Carl cut firewood, his daughter remained in her bedroom, and Theresa sat on the porch, frozen.

The next morning, she went with Carl to a meeting at an attorney's office in town. He explained what had happened. "I would like Theresa to remain with me."

"Her father will need to sign off on that," the man said.

Theresa needed to stay with Carl, who she loved. "I want to stay with my stepfather. I haven't seen my Daddy for a really long time."

The lawyer did not acknowledge her and looked directly at Carl. "I can contact him if you'd like."

Carl nodded and gave him the phone number.

For fifteen long minutes, Carl and Theresa waited silently in the roomy reception area, until the attorney re-emerged from his office. "Theresa's father will not allow you to take custody," he said. "He did give permission for her to stay with Ann's sister, Mable, for the next year. Then she must go to live with her father and stepmother."

Theresa's stomach burned as the dread of reality sunk in. She would have to live with Dorothy.

The days seemed to blur together as Grandma and Carl made arrangements for the funeral. Theresa faced an increasing detachment from everything and everyone. As Theresa dressed for her mother's service, unable to recall the day of the week, she whined about her shoes. "They're too small."

"Stop complaining and do as you're told," Grandma said.

At the church, her grandmother took her hand firmly and led her to the front pew.

Normally, Theresa would enjoy watching the light reflect colors from the stained glass windows, but today, she sat unable to take her eyes from the casket ten feet away. The wood polished to a glossy shine; billowing pillows of golden silk draped from inside the open lid. Theresa stretched taller in her seat trying to see inside, but the coffin was set too high.

The pianist continued turning pages playing hymn after hymn as people filed into the sanctuary. Whenever Grandma wasn't paying attention, Theresa snuck peeks back to the entrance. She recognized faces of firefighters her mother had dressed wounds for, and children whom Ann had taught a decade earlier. Friends and neighbors and shopkeepers. Late-comers squeezed in the pews and leaned against the back wall. Many people Theresa did not know. Ann had been important to all those people—not just her.

Grandma poked Theresa indicating for her to turn around. "It's rude to look backwards in a church," she said.

At the far end of the bench sat Uncle Brad, Aunt Mable, and Theresa's three cousins whom she would soon be living with for a while. Mable held an infant wrapped snugly in a blue cotton blanket. Theresa understood it was her baby brother—half-brother, part of Momma. She looked at the floor, conflicted between hatred towards the child that took her Momma's life and a love for a little boy who would grow up without his mother.

The music finished when the preacher entered the pulpit. "Greetings, in the name of our Lord," he began. "Matthew 5:4 tells us, Blessed are they who mourn, for they shall be comforted."

Theresa folded her arms. She'd never be comforted. The minister went on speaking and reciting more scripture, but she couldn't hear the words. Instead, she kept staring at her mother's pine box. Theresa had not yet been able to shed a tear about her loss as nothing felt real.

Grandma tapped Theresa, holding out a single pink rose. "This is the part we talked about," she whispered. She gave a firm head nod and pushed the reluctant girl up.

Theresa stood and walked slowly to her mother. Inside, Ann lay so peaceful in her favorite green satin dress with delicate white lace at the collar—the one Theresa had helped cut the material for last year.

She swallowed hard, trying to be strong like her mother would expect. "Momma," she whispered. "You look so beautiful." She set the flower on top of Ann's chilly folded hands. Momma was so still.

The pianist began playing the Lord's Prayer. The measure came where Theresa was to begin, but she missed it. She had been practicing the song for the previous few months but she never imagined that the first time she would perform it would be at her own mother's funeral.

"Don't forget to sing to me," Theresa remembered Ann telling her the last time she saw her mother alive. "You have such a pretty voice."

The introduction replayed, and Theresa opened her mouth and her pure young voice filled every last space in the building. She noticed people fighting back their emotions and men offering handkerchiefs to their wives to dab at the corners of their eyes.

After the final Amen was sung, Theresa suddenly felt very, very alone. More alone than at any other time during her life.

Finally, her tears of grief came.

CHAPTER 7
(2006)

"I believe my childhood died on the same day as Momma," said Theresa to her high school interviewers. They both had stopped typing.

"That's so sad," commented Liz, pushing her empty dessert dish to the side. "And to make you see your mom in the coffin and sing—how terrible."

Theresa shrugged. "It's the way things were done in 1947."

Darcy typed a few keystrokes and looked up. "What happened to the baby?"

"A month later, he came to my grandmother's house. I wasn't sure how I'd feel about him. As soon as I held him in my arms, I realized he wasn't to blame. That afternoon, I became rather attached to him. But, I was just beginning to learn the heartaches of loss. My stepfather took the baby and moved back to Texas. Within two months he ended up remarried. They raised my brother to believe that Carl's new wife was his mother."

Liz shook her head. "That seems illegal or something."

Theresa nodded. "Or something. It was a complete betrayal. I did visit when he was ten years old but was threatened not to reveal the truth about his mother, our mother.

"That's lame," said Darcy.

"That didn't sit right with my grandmother, either. She made me promise I'd tell him who our true birth mother was once he turned eighteen. But because he was fighting in Vietnam, I thought it would be too upsetting, so I waited and waited."

She winked at the girls, thinking about how they had put off starting their school interview assignment. "I'm a bit of a procrastinator, myself." Darcy and Liz smiled.

"Did he ever find out?" asked Liz.

"Leave it to Grandma. She took things into her own hands and when she passed away, the will she left forced me to find him to deliver half of her estate. Then it all came out."

Darcy chuckled. "I bet he was totally shocked."

"Yes, indeed. We spent two emotional hours catching up on our lost childhood."

Liz sipped her cold coffee. "Amazing he didn't figure it out sooner."

Theresa raised her hands. "It was much easier to keep secrets in those days. No Internet, no social media. Inconvenient or damning details were simply not spoken about—just tucked away."

From her backpack, Liz retrieved her laptop power cord and plugged it into a wall outlet. "How'd it go living at your aunt's house?"

"Yeah, and with your wicked stepmother?" added Darcy.

Theresa cocked her head. "I was allowed to take one doll, the Bible from Grandpa, and one storybook. I had to leave everything else behind, including my dog, Vicky. I didn't have a stepfather or big stepsister anymore. Momma was gone and there was no baby brother that she'd promised. Daddy hadn't written to me in months and even forgot my birthday that year."

She remembered telling God every night how He had failed her and that He wasn't real. It was a good thing He was patient.

"There simply was no place for me," Theresa said.

CHAPTER 8
(1947 - 1948)

Aunt Mable and Uncle Brad lived in the city. A place that provided Theresa no forest in which to wander, no trees to climb, no cliff to throw rocks over, no river to pan gold in, and no Julianna.

Her oldest cousin Barbara, who was also eleven, didn't even pretend to be interested in exploration or gardening or looking up at the stars.

One stifling afternoon, Mable drove as Brad napped in the passenger seat of their green Chrysler New Yorker. All four children sat squished in the back seat—their sweaty bodies touching and itching. The heat and dust from the road poured in the open back windows.

"Have you ever gone frogging with Grandpa?" Theresa asked her cousins.

"Ewww!" exclaimed nine-year-old Jerry.

Five-year-old Dennis leaned forward. "What's that?"

"It's when you go at night to a swamp and find frogs—"

"Why would you want to go to such a nasty place?" asked Barbara.

Theresa shrugged her shoulders. "Who wouldn't want to explore a swamp?"

"I don't think—" Jerry started.

"I wanna do that," interrupted Dennis. "I'm gonna make Grandpa take me next time."

Barbara shook her head and pushed Dennis further away. "You're too young."

"Am not."

"Are too!"

Mable sighed. "You kids need to be quiet."

The children stopped arguing for a few moments.

Jerry acted somewhat intrigued. "What do you do with the frogs?"

"You chop off their legs and eat 'em," said Theresa.

Barbara poked Theresa's arm. "Shut up. That's so disgusting."

Dennis bounced in his seat. "I wanna eat a frog."

"Shut up!" said Barbara covering her ears and pushing her elbows out in the tight quarters.

Mable raised her voice. "I said, stop. That's enough."

Again, there was silence for a bit until Theresa looked at Dennis, rubbed her tummy, and licked her lips.

He let out a snort, followed by uncontrollable laughter.

The shoving and complaining broke out again until Mable pulled the car to the side of the deserted highway. "Out."

All four children sat frozen, staring at her.

She motioned with her finger. "You heard me. Out."

Having seen her aunts' anger on a few occasions, Theresa avoided talking back or making eye contact with her hoping to avoid any wrath.

Jerry opened the back door and they each crawled out and stood on the gravel. Mable nodded at Barbara, who slammed the door closed. With horror, they heard the clunk of the gear shift and watched Mable drive away.

"Where's she going?" asked Dennis, his eyes growing watery. "Mommy?"

Barbara turned to Theresa. "This is all your fault." She took her youngest brother's hand and began walking. Theresa trailed behind all three of them, feeling a bit rebellious. When Dennis glanced back once in a while, Theresa patted her stomach until he giggled.

After at least an hour, they spotted Mable's car parked by a clump of trees, her husband's head still leaning against his seat. They arrived at the vehicle, opened the door, and climbed in without a peep. Mable said nothing. She completed the letter she was writing, started the car, and resumed driving. Not a word was spoken.

Theresa saw Uncle Brad use one eye to peek at his solemn-faced children. In the rearview mirror, she saw Aunt Mable's face —the tiniest of smiles at the corners of her mouth.

A week before school, Mable took all the children shopping. Barbara, Jerry, and Dennis received many new outfits. Theresa remained patient, believing her turn would come. But she only received new underwear, her first bra—after begging for it, socks, and one pair of shoes.

Everyone marched in the house with armfuls of sacks except for Theresa, carrying her single bag. She cut off all the store labels and put her items away.

Barbara entered and pulled her cousin to her bedroom. "Come help me. We need to take out all the old stuff."

Theresa removed each article of clothing and held it up for either a nod—return to the closet, or a grimace—throw it on the bed. The same task repeated for the dresser drawers. All the while, Barbara hung and folded her new clothes neatly.

Once finished, Barbara nodded at the pile. "You can take whatever you want." Then she disappeared out of the room as Jerry walked in.

"Here, my mom said to give these to you since they don't fit me anymore." He held out some pants and Theresa accepted them. She knew if she didn't, there would be nothing for her to wear outside to play.

He left as she began to sort through his sister's used clothing, choosing what wasn't stained or ripped at the seams. She fought back her tears. Momma had always bought her new school clothes.

Theresa adjusted to sixth grade and a life without all she had loved before. She liked a few of her classmates, but none of them could replace Julianna. Often her cousins skipped out on their daily household chores, and to avoid enduring the resulting arguments, Theresa stepped in to complete them without complaint. She devoured every adventure book she could read escaping her reality by slipping into a world of make-believe.

Despite her difficulties while staying at her aunt's home, after the school year ended, Theresa experienced a sadness about leaving. An unsettled feeling she had begun to recognize. This was her life. Always saying good-bye. Time with her father might be nice but not living with his wife. Momma had despised Dorothy. She would too. At the station, she clung to Aunt Mable. "I want to stay with you."

Mable stroked her niece's hair. "I know, dear. Your father insists that it's time for you to move home."

"I don't like Dorothy."

"I'm sure everything will be fine once you come to know her." Theresa shook her head, doubtful. "You'd better go now."

They hugged again. "Good-bye, Aunt Mable."

"Bye-bye, dear."

Theresa boarded the bus, placed her suitcase on the overhead shelf, and sat by the window gazing out as her aunt waved and drove away. She settled in for the long ride.

"May I sit here?"

Theresa noticed the old lady asking had sparkly eyes. "Sure."

The woman situated herself. "Are you traveling far?"

"All together, about ten hours."

"That is a long trip."

They chatted for a good part of the journey along the winding mountain roads and long straight highways. The lady shared stories of her children and grandchildren and Theresa told her about past summertime camping trips.

"Tell me about your family," the lady invited.

Theresa explained all about her mother dying and her baby brother moving away. She liked how the woman actually appeared interested in her woeful story and so she pressed a little further—crossing over into a more fantasy-type tale. She gave a thoughtful pause. "I have an awful stepmother."

The lady seemed concerned. "Goodness."

Satisfied with her listener's reaction, Theresa continued with the charade. "She's really mean. You should see the bruises on my back."

The woman frowned. "Oh my."

"She forces me to work all the time and sometimes feeds me only bread and water like in Oliver Twist."

"Sounds like a horrible place to live."

"Terrible," Theresa said staving off the guilty feelings and enjoying the rare undivided attention. The woman appeared sorry for her. She listened patiently while responding with empathetic expressions and sympathetic comments. They pulled into the Reno station and Theresa scooted past to exit.

"Take care of yourself," said the lady as she gathered her belongings.

"Thanks," said Theresa, pleased with all her creative storytelling.

The next bus would deliver her to her new home in the small town of Susanville in northern California. After selecting a seat by herself, she noticed the old lady walking up the aisle. Theresa hadn't bothered to ask where she was going. What happened if she got off at the same place? What happened if she knew her father?

Looking down, Theresa began chewing her fingernails, refusing to acknowledge the woman who sat a couple rows behind her.

After two and a half worry-filled hours, Theresa stepped off the bus, dreading the thought of seeing her stepmother. Dorothy approached but offered no friendly smile or warm hug. "Is this your only suitcase?"

"Yes."

As Theresa peered back, her face flushed as the old lady disembarked and walked directly towards Dorothy. "Oh no," Theresa muttered.

"Dorothy," the old lady said. "Nice to see you, again."

"Hello," said Dorothy, and the two women embraced.

The woman smiled and continued. "I have never enjoyed such a ride in all my life. Theresa entertained me all the way here. I barely even realized we were on the bus for so long. She will undoubtedly be an author someday because she tells stories so well." She winked at Theresa.

Theresa gave the woman a small, sheepish smile. Things could have turned out much worse. She'd have to be more careful.

The journey home remained silent. As they drove up the long drive to the house, Theresa considered that she might actually like this place. The house was surrounded by a large ranch with horses and cows grazing in lush pastures. The enormous red barn looked inviting. So much to explore.

Theresa got out of the car and one of the farm dogs ran up to give her a welcome sniff. "Hey boy," she said as he willingly accepted a deep scratch behind his ears.

One of the workers gave a whistle, and the loyal animal took off.

Without a word, Dorothy led Theresa up the stairs and into a bedroom located in the eves of the old house. Blue and yellow curtains bordered the window, a new bedspread covered the bed with a matching dressing table skirt. The room was small but comfortable with one wall slanting up to the A-frame.

Theresa put her suitcase on the bed and walked to the paned glass to see the property stretched out before her. Yes, so much to explore.

Dorothy came up behind her, speaking firmly. "This is a working ranch. You are not to go anywhere around the barn. You are not to talk to the cowboys or ask to ride any horses. You must stay in the front or side yards of the house."

Even while staying with her cousins, Theresa had been allowed to come and go with few questions. She rolled her eyes and turned to set her stepmother straight on a few things. "At my aunt's house, I didn't have any restrictions on where I could—"

Dorothy slapped Theresa's face. "Don't you ever talk back. When I say something, it is not to be questioned."

Theresa touched her reddened cheek. Her stepmother turned and strode out, leaving the girl holding back instant anger. How dare she do that to her.

"You wait until I tell my father," she whispered under her breath.

No invitation to dinner was offered, and she sulked in her room all evening, not caring about her hunger. After crawling into bed, her father entered.

"Hi, Daddy," she said without excitement. She hadn't seen him for so long, but didn't feel like hugging him. How could he have married such a rotten person?

He sat on her bed. "Theresa."

Before he could say anything further, she blurted out what had happened. "Then, she slapped me. Momma never slapped my face."

"Maybe she needed to," he said. "Dorothy is your mother, now."

She scowled. "Dorothy will never be my mother."

Harold stood. "Theresa, stop referring to her as Dorothy. She is your mother and you will call her that. Whatever your mother says is what you must do, and I will not interfere with her raising you." Then he left her alone.

Theresa buried her face in the pillow and sobbed. First, she had lost Momma, and now Daddy, too. After exhausting herself and with no tears left, she flipped to the pillow's dry side and fell asleep. Sleep always helped—at least temporarily.

CHAPTER 9
(1949 - 1950)

Harold and Dorothy had a young child of their own, another half-brother for Theresa. But they kept him away from her as much as possible, and he was spoiled, always hogging all the attention.

After a few months on the ranch, her father and Dorothy decided to move to a nearby city. Theresa disliked cities and much preferred the smaller towns of the mountains, but worst of all, it meant beginning seventh grade in another new school.

Theresa did her best not to request anything from Dorothy, and she certainly disliked calling her 'Mother,' but halfway through that year, she had no choice. She approached Dorothy who was seated at the table reading. "Excuse me, Mother? I think I've started my menses. Do you have any pads?"

With a heavy sigh, Dorothy put down her book and walked to the cupboard below the kitchen sink. Theresa washed dishes every night and was certain there was nothing in there to help in the situation. After removing some old rags, Dorothy held them out. "Here, use these. Pads are too expensive for you." Theresa didn't move. "Go on. Take care of yourself. And for heaven's sake, be careful of the towels."

Stunned, Theresa accepted the rags, said nothing further and returned to the bathroom. Behind the closed door, she stood and cried. How could that woman be so heartless?

For summer months, Theresa stayed with Mable's family where the days were more pleasant and relaxed. Annual camping trips filled with hiking on mountain trails, swimming in chilly lakes, and roasting marshmallows at night.

On one visit, as Theresa and her three cousins hosed out trash cans to earn a few nickels from Uncle Brad, a couple began carrying moving boxes into the home across the street. The tall, attractive young woman saw Theresa watching and waved, her smile bright.

Soon, they all met. Jackie and Ben were ten years older than Theresa, but Jackie took a special liking to her, and they spent time together whenever they could. Theresa thought Jackie was the best listener she knew and she told her about everything.

After arriving back home from Aunt Mable's before ninth grade started, Theresa learned of an amateur talent show being put on by the town. The grand prize being a new wardrobe provided by a retailer in Reno. Knowing no new clothes would come from Dorothy, Theresa decided to enter to win them instead. She practiced singing after school for weeks until the evening of the contest.

Wearing another one of her cousin Barbara's castoff dresses, Theresa shivered on the night walk to the center of town; the fall leaves turning color and the temperatures growing colder. She arrived to the dimmed lights of the theatre and waited patiently along with the other contestants. Her teeth chattered from the chill of the air and also with apprehension. Finally, the master of ceremonies enthusiastically introduced the next performer.

Polite clapping came from the audience when Theresa walked on stage in front of the packed house. Everyone stared, waiting. Her stomach bubbled with nerves. Could she do this? What if she couldn't do this?

Looking up to the spotlight above the projection booth, she heard her mother clearly. "You have such a pretty voice. Sing to me."

Suddenly, a warmth flushed over her and she nodded to the pianist to begin. Theresa's confident voice bellowed out the lyrics to *Somewhere Over the Rainbow*. She sang to her Momma and her Momma alone. On the final note, she closed her eyes and delivered it long and strong.

Thunderous applause caused her eyes to open, and she managed a slight curtsy. For the remainder of the performances, she sat backstage on a stepladder until the host announced the winners—third to a young man who played the guitar; second to a girl who danced; and first place to Theresa. She stood by the side of the stage with her eyes closed. "Thank you for helping me, Momma." Someone gave her a little push and Theresa reentered the stage to collect her prize.

She walked home, mulling over how she would ever tell her parents because there was no way she could claim her winnings without them. Maybe they'd be happy they didn't have to buy her any clothes.

Theresa used the back kitchen door where Harold and Dorothy stood waiting.

Her father did not appear pleased. "Where have you been?"

"I sang in the talent show."

"Did you ask permission from your mother?" he demanded.

Her stepmother folded her arms and shook her head. "No, she did not."

Hoping to avoid the impending punishment, Theresa held up the certificate. "I won first place. This is for a whole bunch of new clothes."

Dorothy snatched the paper from Theresa's hand. "This shop is in Reno. We are not driving you two hours to get clothing."

"But I don't have enough for this year, and they're *free*."

Dorothy folded and tucked the certificate in her pocket. "I'll handle it."

No more conversation about the unclaimed prize occurred. A few weeks later, her father, stepmother, and half-brother made a trip to Reno for the weekend. Surely, they would bring Theresa something home. But when they returned, there were no new clothes for her. She wore her old ones to school that year.

CHAPTER 10
(2006)

"Such a bit...witch," said Liz, catching herself.

"Totally," agreed Darcy. "She probably got new clothes for herself."

"I don't know." Theresa fought the urge for a cigarette. "The next summer when I returned home, my father and stepmother were just finishing packing to move. This meant another new school."

"Again?" said Liz. "You were, like, moving all the time."

"Just about every year. That time I decided to complain rather loudly to Dorothy. Unfortunately, my father heard and he came into the kitchen very upset."

"'Shut up and turn around,' he told me. His tone was terrifying, so I did as he said and he took ahold of my long braid of hair. I knew he was either going to jerk me around or hit me, but instead, I heard a rustling and then felt tugging. Using his pocket knife, he cut off my braid right at my neck, and handed it to me."

"Oh, my gosh. That's so not right," exclaimed Darcy.

"What a..." Liz stopped herself, again.

Theresa's rage had kept her from crying that day, but inside, the hate for her father had swelled. A hardness filled Theresa's chest. So many years had passed and she still felt angry about her father's action that day. Her hair had been the only thing that made her feel pretty, especially the waves created after pulling out the band. "Then my stepmother sat me on a chair and trimmed the rest of my hair with kitchen scissors."

Liz shook her head. "And, I'm sure they made you move, anyway."

"Of course. Dorothy made the living conditions at the new house very clear to me. It was obvious that I'd play little part in their lives."

CHAPTER 11
(1952 - 1953)

Theresa's stepmother led Theresa into the new home in Visalia, California. In the family room, Dorothy walked to a closed door with a padlock on it. She slipped in a silver key and the lock disengaged with a click. Then she swung open the door and they took two steps down into a screened-in porch.

"This is your room. In the winter, you can put those up." She motioned at removable windows leaning against the wall.

Furniture included a twin bed, dresser with a table lamp, dressing table, and one chair. There was a small closet and a tiny enclosed area with a toilet and wash basin. A single door gave access to the outside.

"You can use the washtub on the back patio and hang your clothes on the line, but they are to be taken down as soon as they're dry," said Dorothy. "Your undergarments need to be hung in your bedroom."

Theresa sat hard on the bed and folded her arms, refusing to look at the woman barking out the rules.

"You've got a separate entrance," she nodded to the exterior door. "You are never to use the front door to the house. If you must come inside, you use this door." She pointed at the one with the padlock.

Already knowing the answer, Theresa asked. "Do I get a key?"

"No." Dorothy moved back towards the house. "You will clean the house on Saturday mornings and be finished by noon. Now that you're sixteen, you must find a job and buy your own food."

"Can I use—"

"You will eat in your room."

"But, there's no—"

Dorothy whirled around. "Be grateful you have a roof." She reentered the house and closed the door.

Theresa flopped back on her bed. She couldn't wait to be eighteen so she could leave and they could be rid of her for good. It didn't matter how hungry she got, she would never ask that woman for food.

The next day, Theresa found work at Newberry's, the local five-and-dime store, working behind the soda counter. That night she called Grandma. "Can I please borrow ten dollars? I promise to pay you back as soon as I get paid."

"How are you getting on?" her grandmother asked. "Things any better?"

"Everything's always horrible here. I wish I could live with you or Aunt Mable."

"I know, dear. I'm so sorry your father won't allow it. I'll send the money in the mail, today."

With that money, Theresa purchased bread and juice and made it last for almost three weeks until she received her first paycheck. She also bought a hot plate and small pot with which to cook, although, she kept them hidden in case Dorothy didn't approve.

Carrying her schoolbooks and a paper sack, Theresa, now almost seventeen, walked up her driveway and noticed her parent's car missing. Maybe she could sneak in the house and use the bath. Soaking in a warm tub sounded wonderfully appealing compared to her usual sponge baths in the sink.

She entered her chilly room, placed everything on her bed, and tried the door handle to go into the house. It was locked. A note taped to the door read, 'Back in two weeks.' That meant, no access to the house. No real surprise.

From the grocery bag, she removed a half dozen potatoes—the mainstay of her diet being they were filling and affordable. At least working at the soda counter ensured her a sandwich and soft drink on the four days she worked. Sneaking leftover food off the plates of decent-looking customers became another way to fill her belly.

She peeled a potato, cut it in chunks, and dropped it in a pan of boiling water on her hot plate. Placing her face over the steam and closing her eyes, she recalled the old lady on the bus trip several years earlier and all the exaggerated and fabricated child abuse stories. Theresa chuckled. They hadn't turned out to be too far off.

Theresa pushed a fork in one of the potato pieces. It slid in easily so she poured out most of the water. Boiled or mashed? She added salt and pepper and mashed the potato with the remaining moisture. Theresa remembered peeling potatoes at her grandmother's house as a child and how Grandma had graciously used her rationed butter and milk to make them creamy and delicious. With no refrigeration, those were luxuries Theresa could not afford.

The girl sat on the bed eating her bland dinner and looking at the photograph of her and her mother standing in front of their garden, strawberries abundant on the bushes behind them. "I miss you, Momma."

One Saturday morning when Dorothy was gone, Theresa dutifully mopped the kitchen while her father sat in the family room perusing the newspaper. As the floor dried, she debated if she should ask her father for a little extra money. She had been working at Newberry's as many hours as possible and saving as much as she could. Perhaps with her stepmother gone, he might be more receptive to her request for a few dollars.

Theresa walked in and sat down across from him. "Good morning, Daddy."

He continued his reading. "Morning."

"I'm going to a hayride next weekend. Could you help me with money for a pair of Levis to wear?"

"Is it with those church people?" he said, looking up.

Theresa nodded, knowing he didn't approve of the congregation that had befriended his daughter, providing her a surrogate family.

"No. Your mother said you have too many clothes in your closet now. If you want jeans, it will be out of your own money."

Immediately, Theresa stood, pursuing her lips. Why had she even bothered to ask?

"You know, Theresa," Harold said. "You'll never amount to anything more than a dime store girl."

She wanted to scream in protest, yell at her father that he was wrong. Yet she simply disappeared into the kitchen saying nothing further. Pacing to dissipate her anger, she vowed to prove to him that she could succeed. He would take those words back.

CHAPTER 12
(2006)

"My father and I didn't talk for over a year after that," said Theresa to Darcy and Liz. She shrugged. "There were some enjoyable times with friends, but never at home. I'm sure I wasn't the perfect little angel, either."

Darcy drank the last of her coffee. "Well, probably because they were so mean to you."

"Once in a while, Dorothy and I would converse in a civil manner, but I kept my distance. She did sew me a graduation dress. I think because she knew I'd be leaving soon."

Liz shook her head. "What an awful childhood. I thought I had it bad in my family."

Theresa picked up her purse. "How about a five-minute break?"

"Yeah," agreed Liz. "I gotta use the bathroom."

"Are you alright, Ms. Clavin?" Darcy asked.

"Just need a little fresh air," Theresa said and exited the shop. She walked to the side of the building, fumbled out a cigarette, and lit up. Childhood had been difficult. Yet, at her age now, she must admit it had made her stronger. Made her into someone able to keep pushing forward through any adversity. Through the window, she saw the girls waiting for her so she extinguished her cigarette and went back inside.

Once back in her seat, Theresa continued. "My father's words about not amounting to anything got me through the rest of high school and my start in college. I was determined to get through it all, if for no other reason than to prove him wrong."

"And did you?" Darcy asked.

"You bet your booty, I did. After high school, I moved out and rented an apartment with a friend. I enrolled in night classes at junior college—like a community college, nowadays. I worked full time every day to pay for my courses and the rent."

"I'm not going to…" began Liz. She became distracted by watching the boy who had winked at her earlier.

He stood, stretched, and threw away an empty muffin wrapper.

Liz gave him a small wave when he left the coffee shop.

"You were saying?" asked Theresa, her eyebrows raised.

"Um," stammered Liz when she looked back.

Darcy rolled her eyes. "She just wants to get married, but I wanna go to college."

"Good for you, Darcy," Theresa said, then she looked directly at Liz. "I didn't date at all for those first three years in school—just too busy."

"That's pretty lame," said Liz.

"Maybe so, but that didn't mean I didn't *notice* the boys."

They all smiled.

"There was one in particular in my Geology class. Tall, blond hair, blue eyes, muscular—very handsome. I found myself rather dizzy every time I was around Stephen."

"Oh, I know what you mean," said Liz leaning forward.

"He also was an only child. Yet unlike me, his parents spoiled him and he acted so self-assured. The warning signs were there. I was falling for him."

Liz sighed and nodded.

"Stephen and his folks, Joseph and Vye, invited a group of us to go on a summer water ski vacation. Despite the dreadful heat, we camped in tents and had so much fun. His father and mother seemed generous and caring. Stephen was a competitive water skier and he enjoyed showing off his talents as us girls stood on the shore swooning. He held my hand a few times and even kissed me after dinner one night. I was bit."

"Ooooo," the girls crowed together.

"Then, I received some news."

CHAPTER 13
(1957)

Theresa walked into her apartment late on a Thursday night. After working all day at Western Union as a Telegrapher followed by attending evening classes for four hours, her body screamed for sleep. Pushing through her nightly routine, she washed her face, put on her pajamas, and sat down to eat a bowl of cereal while shuffling through the mail on the kitchen table.

The local newspaper which she set to the side.

A thick letter from Jackie, the woman she had met years ago at Aunt Mable's house. Jackie was better at writing letters than Theresa but the two of them continued to nurture their friendship. She read the letter to catch up on her friend's life. They'd have to plan another visit soon.

Theresa continued with the mail—the electric bill, an overdue notice delivered in error and that belonged to her neighbor, and an official gray envelope from Chapman College.

She stopped eating and touched the school's return address. "Please, please, please," she muttered as she slid her finger along the sealed edge to open it. Holding her breath, she removed and unfolded the paper.

At the un-stifled scream, her roommate came running out. "What's wrong?"

Theresa turned, tears streaming down her face. "I got accepted at Chapman College. They gave me a one-year scholarship in the education department."

Her friend hugged her. "Congratulations."

"With this and all I've saved, I can live in a dorm like a real college student. I'll only have to get a job in the summer."

"You've worked so hard for this. I'll miss not seeing you." Theresa frowned. "I know. I never see you anyway," her friend clarified.

They both laughed.

Theresa then phoned Jackie to share the exciting news.

Five weeks later, Theresa rode the bus to her new school, thinking of other bus rides taken back and forth between her father and her aunt's home. She couldn't help but smile at all the years she spent working and saving every penny to fatten up her bank account. Theresa sat up taller in her seat, knowing she was proving to her father that she would amount to something.

Once at the college, Theresa witnessed the bustle of activity going on around her and soon jumped in herself. In the gym, she registered for her upcoming courses. She joined others on a school tour led by a senior student. He explained that Chapman had the highest enrollment in their history at three hundred fifty with almost half living on campus. And she was going to be one of them. Theresa reveled in the reality, unable to wipe the smile from her face.

After the tour, she visited all her scheduled classrooms to meet her teachers. Then, she found the dormitory where she would be living. It was actually one of several big old houses.

A sixty-five-year-old woman with bright white hair and plump, round cheeks, greeted Theresa at the front door. "I'm Mrs. White, the house mother."

She showed Theresa the home that consisted of several bedrooms set up to house twenty-two young women, two or three to a room.

Upon entering a room on the top floor, Mrs. White addressed a woman gazing out of the faded yellow curtains. "Kathleen? This is Theresa. You two will be roommates."

Kathleen turned with a grand, genuine grin. Instantly, Theresa liked her, and they walked around greeting more of the women whom they would spend much of their time with during the next school year.

Theresa knew that Stephen had also transferred to Chapman. Of course, he still lived at home, everything being paid for by his parents. The day ended in the best way possible when she ran into him. He asked her out for coffee and they talked for over an hour about school, classes, and teachers.

On her trip home, she glowed at the fact that she was now Stephen's equal. Soon she'd be a full-time student who wouldn't miss out on everything because of having to work just to make ends meet. Perhaps he and she could actually date. That sounded like a fine idea.

CHAPTER 14
(1957 - 1958)

Suddenly, Theresa had time and friends and a new family. The women living in the house behaved like a typical home full of sisters—laughing, bickering, and talking of handsome men and school work. They would meet in the house parlor for last minute adjustments to their dresses before walking across campus for school dances. Theresa's days and nights brimmed with classes, homework, parties, sporting events, and dating.

Every night she fell into bed exhausted and happy vowing not to miss out on anything. Not a single thing.

Theresa enjoyed the opportunity to get to know the male students in a group setting as it was less intimidating—especially when it came to the dances.

One Saturday night, a large number of her friends attended a school-sponsored dance. The gym was decorated with balloons and streamers, and a disc jockey stood on the stage spinning forty-five's of the latest top-chart hits like, *Whole Lotta Shakin' Going On* and *All Shook Up*. Men and women danced, twisting and bopping. Theresa sat tapping her foot, enjoying the music and watching the crazy antics of the dancers. Whenever asked to dance, she would smile and deliver her standard response, "I've got two left feet, but thank you." Politely, the men would nod and continue down the line finding another woman who was eager to jump out on the floor.

Later in the evening, Theresa saw Tony walking in her direction. Her heart fluttered as he flashed his Elvis Presley smile. He was way too popular to be really interested in her. Even as a sophomore and a year younger than her, he was involved in Chapman College school leadership, and was a star baseball and basketball player. Theresa glanced around thinking he was headed to someone else, but he kept coming at her. He stopped and greeted a couple friends. There was no way he was going to ask her to dance. He had dated some of her roommates and often participated in their group activities. She liked him because he was plain fun to be around, always engaging everyone with his stories and infectious laugh.

Wake Up Little Susie by the Everly Brothers began playing and Tony excused himself from his friends and continued on his path to Theresa.

He arrived with his handsome face and reached out his hand.

"Oh, I've got two left—"

Tony ignored her, grabbed ahold of her hand, and pulled her onto the sleek gym floor where the music pulsated and energetic young adults moved.

"I don't dance," she yelled.

He leaned closer. "What?"

"I can't dance."

He grinned and led her into a spin.

Theresa did her best, and after she stomped on his feet seven times, she stopped counting. But, he didn't seem to care and kept working with her.

After what felt like an eternity, the song ended. She was grateful when Tony gave her a hug, returned her to her seat, and invited another woman to dance. Out of breath, Theresa sat down and drank half her punch at once.

A tall, thin man slipped in the seat next to her. "Thirsty?"

Theresa laughed. "Dancing's never been my thing. He's hard to keep up with."

They looked over and saw Tony swinging his new partner over his back and through his legs.

"I could see that," he said.

She recognized his face. "You're on the basketball team."

He reached to shake her hand. "I'm William."

"Theresa."

"I know."

She tilted her head. Had they already met? "Sorry. There've been so many new people."

"No, we haven't been introduced. But we have a mutual acquaintance."

"Who's that?"

"Jackie."

She was surprised. "How do you know her?"

"Through my ex-wife. I've known Jackie for about four years. She's still a good friend, and my daughter loves her. My daughter lives with her mother."

"Oh," acknowledged Theresa realizing that he had already been married, divorced, and had a child. "Jackie's been a friend of mine for a long time. We met back when I was just a teenager. So, you're back in school now?"

"Yeah. I held down a full-time job for a while, but I came back to finish my degree." He glanced at the dancers and back to Theresa. "Hey, you want to grab some coffee or something?"

Theresa looked at her watch, her eyes widened. She stood and picked up her purse. "Sorry, I can't, William. I have this big history test on Monday and I've got to study."

He stood and smiled. "Maybe another time?"

William seemed like a nice guy, and certainly 'Jackie approved,' although he's already been through so much. She smiled, said goodbye to a couple friends, and left.

Theresa was amused at how often guys would stand in front of the house and serenade the admired young women. One man would hold a guitar as a few others gazed up to the windows and crooned out *You Send Me* and *I Beg of You*. She hoped someday Stephen would want to be more than just friends and come serenade her.

One night, long after Theresa was asleep, she and Kathleen woke at the shrill sound of a whistle. They sat straight up in bed, wondering what was going on. Screams came from all over the house, but before they could react, their bedroom door flung open and in ran two young men throwing something at the frightened women.

Theresa and Kathleen shrieked at the splash of cold water from the breaking water balloons. Now laughing, they were up and out of bed as the boys bolted from the room.

All the female students converged on the stairwell.

Mrs. White also appeared, her breath heavy and face crimson. "You boys get out of here. Get out now," she shouted.

The shocked women, several in soaked nightgowns, watched as their male friends took the stairs two-by-two and sprang out the front door. Some laughed, others chattered, a few were upset.

"I hope she doesn't have a heart attack," Kathleen said, pointing at Mrs. White who held one hand on her chest while shuffling residents back in their rooms. Theresa recognized their house mother did her best to keep things peaceful and 'age-appropriate,' but, between the men's and women's dormitory houses, plenty of mischief took place.

After changing into dry pajamas, Theresa crawled back into her bed, experiencing a warm feeling all over. She no longer was alone.

In the cafeteria a week later, Theresa and Kathleen carried their lunch trays to a table and sat down.

"Have you done the assignment for Mr. Lambin's class, yet?" asked Theresa as she stirred buttered peas into whipped potatoes using a fork. She looked up and saw Kathleen staring wide-eyed at the flower centerpiece on the table.

Draped over the flowers were a pair of pink women's panties with lace designs on the sides.

Theresa gasped, her hand flying over her mouth.

"Those are mine," said Kathleen, horrified.

Turning to look around, Theresa witnessed other lunch-goers appreciating their own unique centerpieces—white ones, green ones, brown ones.

"What on earth?" Then she spotted some of the culprits who were chuckling and looking over. Theresa grinned at their playfulness. "Those boys must've got into our bedrooms."

Kathleen's face reddened, and she massaged her forehead.

Alice, another woman who lived in Theresa's house, approached the table on her way to empty her tray. She nodded at the pink underwear. "I heard they sent some to Nelson's office."

Kathleen looked up. "The school president?"

"Special delivery."

Theresa enjoyed the game playing. They couldn't just let this prank go unanswered as there must be revenge upon the boys. She began devising an idea and presented it to her roommate later that night.

Well after midnight, Theresa and Kathleen snuck into bedrooms in their own house. They 'borrowed' more pairs of underwear from several of their housemate's drawers. Carrying their stash in a small bag, they stealthily exited the house through the back door and half-walked, half-ran to the main campus courtyard.

After seeing no one around, they scurried to the empty flagpole.

"Quick, here, you hand them to me," whispered Theresa. "And keep an eye out."

"OK, but hurry." Kathleen opened the bag and handed over one pair at a time.

Using clothespins, Theresa attached ten pairs. It took a few minutes to finish securing them, then she took hold of the rope and pulled. Dutifully, the panties raised to the top where they flapped in the breeze.

Theresa gave an over-dramatic staunch salute at the red, white, and blue. Kathleen did the same. Then they both burst into laughter. This was beyond fun.

"Shh," warned Kathleen.

"Come on, let's get outta here," said Theresa.

The women ran off, trying to stifle their giggles.

An hour later, Theresa awoke to Kathleen shaking her shoulder. "What's wrong?"

"I think maybe we shouldn't have done it."

"No one will ever know."

"Probably," replied Kathleen. "But, what happens if someone finds out it was us and not the boys?"

Theresa shook her head. "Don't worry so much."

"Think about it. If we're caught, we might be kicked out of school."

Theresa considered that possibility.

"It would be awful," said Kathleen, frowning. "My parents would be so angry."

Getting expelled after working so hard to get into college would definitely give Harold something more to criticize Theresa on. That wouldn't be good. "Do you want to just go and take them down, then?"

Kathleen nodded.

They got dressed and returned to the flagpole. Theresa started pulling on the ropes and the goodies began to descend. At half-mast, everything became tangled.

"Oh no," exclaimed Kathleen. "They're stuck."

The girls tried to untangle the lines, but to no avail.

"Something's snagged," said Theresa, still attempting to work things free. Her heart beat faster as she stepped back to inspect the situation. Next to the pole was a trellis. "I'll climb up and see if I can tell you how to untwist them."

Kathleen groaned.

"Just keep watch." Theresa lifted a nearby trash can and set it by the trellis. She could do it. She'd climbed hundreds of trees before. Stepping on the trashcan, she hoisted herself up on the wooden slats, balanced herself, and leaned over. "Twist this line to the right. No, too far. Try and flip this one away from the other. No, no, the other one."

Kathleen tried following Theresa's directions, but no progress was made. A loud crash came from behind the administration building. The women glanced at each other.

"Come on, Theresa, forget it. Let's go now before someone catches us for sure."

Theresa scrambled back down and the two friends ran back to their house. Had they been seen? Would someone find out? Sleep was restless the remainder of the night.

The next morning, Theresa and Kathleen carried their textbooks and acted as though nothing had happened. Theresa battled a nervous stomach as they rounded the corner, and received a full view of the action in the courtyard. She gulped.

On the perfectly manicured lawn was a fire truck with its ladder extended up the flagpole. The fireman picked panties off the ropes, snickering as he did so. Clusters of students stood around watching and laughing.

Not appearing pleased at all, President Nelson stood back observing. He rolled his eyes as a local newspaper journalist snapped a photograph.

Theresa and Kathleen covered their mouths, stifling their laughter. What an adventure college was turning out to be.

CHAPTER 15
(2006)

"That's hysterical," said Liz, as they all laughed.

"Oh, my gosh," added Darcy. "Did they ever find out it was you guys?"

Theresa shook her head and grinned. "You're the first to know. Everyone assumed it was the boys. The school president did try to lay down the law to curb the panty raids, but boys are boys."

"Maybe I should think again about college. It sounds so cool," claimed Liz.

Theresa wagged her finger at them. "Don't you two get any ideas. In fact, you'll probably want to leave that part out of your school assignment."

Darcy tapped her temple dramatically and raised her eyes. "Hmmmm. I don't think so."

They all chuckled more.

Theresa gazed upwards remembering how she had never enjoyed being a part of something so much. That new found clique-i-ness made her junior year one of the best in her life.

"So, what happened to Stephen, Ms. Clavin?" asked Liz.

"Yes, Stephen. He participated in most of the shenanigans."

Liz shifted to sit cross-legged on her seat. "Did you finally start dating?"

"We went out a couple of times with other couples, but we remained just friends—not my choice. Our college basketball team made it into the finals that year. It was so exciting and in the final seconds, William passed the ball to Tony who dribbled past his opponent, took the shot, and scored, winning the championship. The whole auditorium went nuts. That's when Stephen kissed me in public for the first time."

Darcy typed notes. "How old were you?"

"Almost twenty-two. Stephen began to fill more and more of my thoughts. Granted, I was more serious than he, but I figured he'd come around."

Liz tilted her head. "Did he?"

Theresa smiled. "Through the summer break, I worked to replenish my money. I lived with my grandmother, who didn't live far from Stephen's house. Naturally, I rode my bicycle over as much as I could, even if he wasn't there. I loved his mother, Vye. She often fed me lunch and we went shopping together."

"His mom and dad liked you, then?" said Darcy.

"They certainly acted like it. Eventually, I received the invitation to have dinner. Everything seemed perfect sitting with Stephen and his parents having a real family meal. And I was so in love with Stephen—I knew what I wanted."

CHAPTER 16
(1958)

Towards the end of summer, three weeks before her senior year at college started, Theresa rode her bicycle to Stephen's house as she had many evenings during the previous two months. She propped the bike up with the kickstand and approached the front door. Before knocking, she fluffed her hair and straightened her skirt and blouse. She wondered if he'd notice the new outfit.

Stephen answered, a wide smile spread across his face. "Well, hello."

She beamed back. He was so dreamy. "Hi. I was just on my way home. I need a recipe and want to check with your mother to —"

"Come on in. I'm glad you stopped by." He opened the door.

Theresa entered and he motioned her to the living room couch. "You want something to drink?"

"Sure, thanks. Maybe some of your mom's lemonade?"

Stephen hurried to the kitchen. She pinched her cheeks and applied another layer of lipstick. He seemed pleased to see her, which made her heart pound a little faster.

Minutes later, he carried in two tall glasses and handed her one.

"Thanks. Your mom makes the best." She looked around. "Are your folks home?"

"Not right now."

His intense gaze made her shift in her seat. "So, did you get registered for all the psychology classes you wanted?" she asked.

"Yeah."

"Pick out a graduate school, yet?"

He shook his head while keeping his eyes locked with hers.

"Well, I'm sure wherever it is, you'll do well."

"Yes, I'm sure," he agreed.

Theresa raised her glass to toast. "To your future."

"To my future."

Their glasses clinked. She paused a moment hoping for a reciprocated acknowledgement, one never came, so she took a sip. It didn't matter. Stephen put down his drink and moved nearer. Beads of sweat formed on her forehead, a flutter in her tummy.

"Is that a new top?"

He noticed the shirt. That was good. Theresa felt strangely powerful and confident. "Actually, it is."

"I like it."

"Thank you."

He sniffed at her neck. "And, you smell so fine."

That tickled and she laughed. Her laugh was followed by an awkward pause as she searched for something else to say. "I'm looking forward to starting school again. Are you?"

"Uh-huh."

"I'm able to do some student teaching this year," she said. "That should—"

Stephen leaned over and kissed her. She barely managed to set the glass on the coffee table. She liked that things were definitely turning more serious. Theresa put her arms around him and he gently pushed her back on the sofa.

Back on her bike ninety minutes later, Theresa was glowing. He is the one. She knew after what they had done, Stephen and her would marry after they had graduated from school. He would be a successful psychologist and she would be a teacher, at least up until they had children. Their lives together would be wonderful. She'd have her own beautiful, loving family.

CHAPTER 17
(1958)

A couple weeks passed and Theresa tried not to think about the fact that Stephen had not called her. He must be busy getting ready for school. Surely, he was making plans and searching for possible graduate colleges for next year. They would connect again once school started.

Her summer job ended and she focused on her new opportunity to earn extra money by helping prepare the dormitory for the new year. Her task involved sewing new draperies for all the bedrooms in the house. She carried in two bolts of material. One navy blue and the other with a white and yellow floral pattern. She spread the fabric on the table in the common room of the house, marked it, and began cutting.

While finishing a seam on one panel, the front door opened and she looked up from the machine. Tony stood with a wide grin holding a hammer and container of nails.

"Hello, Tony," she said.

"Hi, Theresa. How was your summer?"

She snipped the thread. "Worked a lot. How about yours?"

He walked closer nodding his head. "Good, good."

"You here to fix the kitchen window?"

"Yeah." Tony pointed at her project. "What are you making?"

"New dorm room curtains."

He rubbed his chin. "Really?"

"Un-huh. Why?"

"Do you think you could make some for my apartment? My roommate has newspaper taped to the window."

She laughed. "I suppose. I'd need to measure and tell you how much fabric you'll have to buy. I'm sure you don't want this." She motioned towards the flowery material.

He shook his head. "Why don't you come by later?"

"Sure."

That evening, Theresa took her tape measure, pad of paper, and pencil to Tony's apartment and knocked.

Tony swung open the door and slurred his elation. "Theresa!"

Smelling alcohol on his breath, she glanced inside and saw newspaper hung haphazardly to the window. Presented on the coffee table was an array of cheese, sausages, and bread. Of more concern was the opened bottle of wine. Theresa squeezed her fingers tighter around the pencil. She rarely consumed alcohol as she didn't fare well with it.

"To thank you, I thought you'd enjoy some snacks and a little refreshment," he said.

Theresa stalled. This was a perfectly innocent offer of hospitality, right?

Tony acknowledged her hesitation. He offered up his usual charm and warmth, and gently took her arm. "Come on. You can't measure the window from out here."

No question that she and Tony were only friends, because she was in love with Stephen, after all. Tony probably had a steady girlfriend anyway being so popular. Theresa had skipped dinner, so what harm could there be in a few bites of meat and cheese while measuring for the curtains? Theresa allowed herself to be led inside, just as he had led her on the dance floor during the last school year.

Tony closed the door and immediately walked to the empty glass next to the bottle, and poured.

"Only a little," she said.

He ignored the request and filled it three-quarters full. "You can't just have a little of this," he said holding out the glass for her. "This is my Grandpa's homemade wine. Here, taste it."

Attempting to remain polite, Theresa accepted and took a sip. A smile of surprise came across her face. "You're right. This is excellent." She took another swallow—the fruity flavor went down easily.

"A recipe straight from Sicily," he said. "He gave me a few bottles."

"So, your family is from Italy?"

He frowned at her playfully. "Bite your tongue. We are from Sicily."

Theresa chuckled, sipped again, and set the strong, yet delicious drink down. She picked up her tape and measured the window dimensions. "You have a large family?"

Tony refilled his glass and walked over to watch and talk. "Started with seven kids, but lost my sister to cancer and my brother at sea."

"I'm so sorry."

He took another gulp. "How about you?"

"I always wanted a big family. Or at least one that stayed together. My mom died when I was young so I lived with my father and stepmother. There was a stepsister, but we didn't get along."

Theresa shut her notepad.

"Got everything you need?"

She nodded.

He motioned her to the couch with a hand wave and low bow. "Well, have something to eat. I slaved in the kitchen all afternoon."

Theresa laughed at his animated hand gesture and facial expression. After topping off her wine, they spent a good part of the evening chatting about their favorite classes and teachers. They discussed their lives and their future plans. She enjoyed his amusing sense of humor, and his genuine interest in her life, something Stephen neglected to do much of. Somewhere in there, a second bottle was uncorked. By the time he kissed her, the bottles stood empty and she was drunk. The moments eluded her.

Later, Theresa found herself stumbling to the church one block off campus. One where she went many a late night in search of quiet time. She sat in the front pew of the modest, deserted sanctuary watching candles flicker on the altar. An ominous shadow of darkness cast across one of the stained glass windows due to an extinguished light bulb.

Her memory of the previous couple of hours was sketchy and some parts were completely blank. She felt dizzy and nauseous. Where had her mind gone? She didn't recall exactly what had taken place, but her body gave her the evidence. Her skirt and blouse were askew and her face felt flushed.

Theresa sat motionless, her hands clasped, and head swirling with scary thoughts. She hoped Tony would not speak of her visit to his apartment. If Stephen found out, for certain there would be no future for them together. She cried. She must not tell anyone, not a soul. Everyone liked Tony. No one would believe what happened because she drank too much stupid wine.

"Momma?" Theresa whispered. She heard nothing. "You said you'd be with me. Are you there? Momma?" Just silence.

Through her tears she prayed, but God was missing, too. Alone again. All by herself with her guilt and shame.

The next day she finished the drapes for the dorm rooms. With the leftover blue fabric, she sewed Tony's request and went hoping she might gain some reassurance that their encounter would stay between them. He wasn't hard to find in the crowd at the local malt shop. Through the window, she observed him suck down a chocolate shake and greet friends. Theresa imagined the lively conversation of everyone sharing their summer vacation adventures and plans for the upcoming school year.

With her stomach tied in knots, she remained outside. After a while, people filed out, still chattering. She stood twenty feet from the entrance and when Tony exited he saw her and walked over.

"How are you feeling?"

Her face reddened. "I don't handle alcohol—"

Tony made a zipping motion across his lips and winked. She could trust him.

Theresa handed over his curtains. "I hope these work."

"But, I was supposed to buy—"

"It's fine. I had leftover material."

He reached into his back pocket and pulled out his wallet. "They're cool. Let me—"

"No, that's okay."

One of the senior cheerleaders called out. "Tony, you coming?"

He waved at her. "Yeah." He looked back to Theresa, raised the folded fabric in hand, and tilted his head. "Thanks."

She turned and walked in the other direction exhaling a long, controlled breath. That harsh lesson could now be put behind her. No more drinking. Maybe God had been listening after all.

CHAPTER 18
(1958)

On the third day of school, Theresa saw Stephen walking towards her on campus. Her chest pounded as he approached. She smiled broadly, but he did not stop to talk. He gave a casual smile and friendly nod as he passed on by. He was acting like before—just friends. She didn't understand.

Theresa sat in class not hearing anything of the professor's lecture. Maybe she could make an excuse to go by Stephen's house. Or find him later after classes. Perhaps she should call him. But, girls don't call boys. Did Tony say anything about what happened? She felt certain that wasn't the problem. No, she had been too willing for Stephen, too easy to sweep off her feet. Her heart ached. She wasn't good enough. Her recently-found confidence and power melted away, replaced by her old friend—anger.

She stared at William sitting near the front of the room and devised her plan. The bell rang and she walked up to him and accepted his long-standing offer for coffee. Perhaps Stephen would witness them together, and develop some jealousy.

Despite finding William mature and nice to talk with, she made her intentions clear. "I don't really want to date."

William shrugged. "So, we'll be friends."

Theresa enjoyed his refreshing attitude and understood why people liked him.

But her scheme did not work. Stephen still did not call although he was quite visible on campus, talking and flirting with other women.

She walked from the library back to her dorm late at night. Going to study there had not been productive, as her thoughts revolved around Stephen. She remembered the first time he held her hand and their first kiss. With a small smile but heavy eyes, she thought of the dinners with his parents and how at home she felt. Then, making love with Stephen. She allowed herself a few moments of recalling how wonderful that feeling of closeness had been. And now what does she have? Nothing.

Theresa entered her room where her roommate already lay snoring. She quietly slipped into bed, exhausted, but knowing she wouldn't sleep. How could she have been so wrong about Stephen? Why didn't he have the same love for her? Her nightly tears rolled down to wet her pillow once again. She had just been stupid and now she must face the truth. He got what he wanted from her, and had moved on to his next conquest.

Sniffing, she turned on her back and clenched her jaw as she stared up into the darkness. Theresa would not allow Stephen to bring her down. She was stronger than that. She decided focusing solely on academics during her final year of school would be her best distraction and the way to move forward.

CHAPTER 19
(1958)

A month after her senior year began, Theresa was sitting in the college doctor's office.

"I need something to start my period," she told the elderly man.

"Why is that?"

"I've been under so much stress with school and everything." She didn't mention her heartbreak over Stephen and her lack of sleep.

He nodded and gave her a shot. Theresa didn't care what it was.

A week later she was back. "It didn't work, can I please get another one?"

Reluctantly, he complied. "Now, you must go home and get some rest."

She slowly got up not wanting to admit to herself that her situation could be anything more than just not enough rest. The thoughts of what might be possible were shoved from her mind. Don't think it, and it won't be true.

In her modern dance class, Theresa put herself in all sorts of unnatural contortions. Pushing and twisting, jumping and falling.

One of her classmates watched, shaking her head. "How do you do that?"

Later, Theresa ran up the stairs at the house full speed, almost knocking Kathleen over on the way.

"Whoa, slow down," said Kathleen. "You're going to hurt yourself."

Theresa knew her friend was exactly right as she willed her body to reject what might be inside.

Still her period did not start and one afternoon she finally faced it straight on. Using the hall phone in the house, she called the one person she knew would help. "I might be in trouble."

Thirty minutes later, Jackie picked up her friend and waited patiently for her to reveal the issue. At first, Theresa was afraid to verbalize her suspicions from the past few weeks, but as the silence grew longer, she uttered the words aloud for the first time. "I think I'm pregnant."

Jackie immediately pulled the car over. She put her arms around Theresa, who couldn't think or reason, only release the tears that came in waves.

All the while, Jackie rubbed her friend's back. "We'll figure things out. I promise."

Theresa cried until her face was red and puffy, and only sniffles remained. Jackie started the vehicle and headed to her home. Theresa listened to her friend schedule an appointment with her doctor for the next day. Barely past sunset, Jackie helped Theresa into the guest bed where she fell into a heavy slumber.

The following morning, sitting on the examination table inside a stark white room, Theresa closed her eyes. "God, please make the news good."

A middle-aged woman entered the room. "Hello Theresa, I'm Dr. Roberts."

"What are the results?"

The doctor seemed pleased to deliver the news. "Congratulations, you're going to have a baby."

Theresa tried to process the doctor's words. She was pregnant.

"So, we'll need to start you on—"

"No, no, no. This can't be," interrupted Theresa. Of course, she knew exactly how that could be. Putting her face in her hands, she closed her eyes and took a deep breath.

"Well dear, the test doesn't lie."

Theresa snapped her head up. "No, you don't understand. I cannot be pregnant."

"But—"

"I'm not married yet. And, I have to finish school. This can't happen."

The doctor nodded her head. "I see."

"Isn't there something you can do?"

"I'm sorry. Perhaps you can talk to the father," suggested Dr. Roberts.

Theresa cried out in frustration. "You don't get it. There's got to be something you can do. I can't have this baby." The eye contact she gave the physician was steady and deliberate.

"Abortion is illegal, Theresa."

"I know that. But I'm desperate. Please help me."

"Look, I can't—"

"Please, Dr. Roberts."

The doctor stared blankly at her for an extended moment, then clenched her jaw. She tore a blank section of paper off her prescription pad, scribbled something and shoved it towards Theresa. Saying nothing further, she left the room.

Theresa looked at the phone number and slipped it in her pocket, praying she wouldn't need it. She found Jackie in the waiting room. Once back in the car, Theresa confirmed she was expecting.

"What do you think Stephen will say?" Jackie asked.

Theresa stared out the window. It made logical sense the baby was Stephen's. Tony was just a little misstep. She had slept with Stephen first and he remained the man that she loved, even though he obviously did not feel the same about her. Might this make a difference to him?

"What are you going to do?"

"I don't know, but I can't talk about it, yet."

They rode in silence back to Theresa's house.

"Thank you for taking me."

"Of course," said Jackie. "Call me when you're ready."

Theresa got out and began walking away.

Jackie called from the car window. "You really need to tell someone in your family so they can help you make a decision."

Theresa shook her head and walked away. No one would understand. What could she do?

For days, she immersed herself in school work. She studied early in the morning and late in the night. Time in between classes was spent in the library, reading and writing. Every moment was filled to avoid thinking about her body or the one inside of it. At bedtime, she fell asleep quickly. Sleep had always been her way to step out of reality.

By the next week, Theresa could no longer distract herself. Things needed to be dealt with as it wouldn't go away just because she ignored it. She called Jackie. "You're right. Someone in my family needs to know."

"Who?"

It would be unbearable to hear her father say he was right. That she hadn't amounted to anything. "I can't tell my father and Dorothy. And my Grandma would be so disappointed."

"How about your aunt and uncle," suggested Jackie.

"That's my only option."

"You can do it at my house if you'd like. Your cousins probably don't need to be around."

Theresa wanted as few people to be aware of her predicament as possible. "Can you call and see if we can meet this Saturday?"

Jackie agreed and made the arrangements.

Through her embarrassment, Theresa explained her problem to Aunt Mable and Uncle Brad. They didn't say much but recognized why she had chosen to involve them. Brad phoned Stephen's father, and within the hour, Theresa and her aunt and uncle were on their way over.

Theresa convinced herself that even though the circumstances were in no way ideal, perhaps Stephen and his parents would understand. They had liked her and always treated her kindly, almost like one of the family. Maybe something good might still come from this with Stephen.

CHAPTER 20
(1958)

Theresa followed behind Aunt Mable and Uncle Brad as they approached the house. Drowning in humiliation, she clenched her teeth and tried to breathe normally.

Stephen's father answered the door somberly and shook Brad's hand. "Please, come in."

"This is my wife, Mable."

Joseph nodded at her as she trailed behind her husband. When he saw Theresa, there was no greeting, just a disgusted scowl. He turned his back to her and walked away leaving her alone to close his front door. The same door where she had been so warmly welcomed many times before. Theresa got a sick feeling.

In the living room, Stephen's mother, Vye, met her new guests. She said nothing to Theresa, but patted her gently on the back. At least she might understand.

They all sat on the couch and chairs, Theresa by herself on one side of a loveseat.

"Lemonade?" offered Vye.

"Stephen?" Joseph bellowed towards the stairway.

Theresa's heart beat faster.

Mable nodded. "Yes, thank you." Vye poured the drinks from a pitcher already placed on the coffee table.

Joseph yelled louder. "Stephen?"

Theresa closed her eyes at his thunderous voice. She wondered if he had told Stephen about Uncle Brad's phone call and the reason for their visit.

Stephen's voice came from upstairs. "Yeah?"

"I need you down here, now," Joseph demanded.

Theresa's hands trembled so she tucked them under her legs. With every footstep coming down the stairs, she grew more nervous.

Stephen entered the room wearing jeans and a favorite Chapman College tee shirt. His hair was unruly and his face unshaven, obviously not expecting company. Theresa wished she could be anywhere else but there.

He looked around, surprised to see everyone staring at him. "What's going on?"

Joseph motioned his son into the room, then crossed his arms. "Apparently, Theresa is pregnant and claiming it's your child."

Stephen's face went white and he looked at her. "It can't be."

Theresa frowned at him. *He's not going to admit it?*

He ran his hand across his head and exhaled. "Are you sure?"

She nodded, and he stared at the floor in disbelief.

Joseph took charge of the conversation. "Well, we need to examine our options here."

"Our next-door neighbor's daughter had this happen," said Mable. "She ended up moving away to have the baby and has been struggling ever since to raise it by herself."

"Perhaps marriage—" started Stephen's mother, giving Theresa a small smile.

"No," Joseph interrupted. He glared at his wife, who said no more, having been corrected. "If Stephen gets married, he will have to quit school and go to work because we will not pay for him to finish college and support a family as well."

Theresa leaned forward. "What about working and going to school at night? I did that for three—"

"No. That's not possible," said Stephen.

She sat back in her seat folding her arms and refusing to look at him.

Theresa and Stephen remained silent while listening to a discussion about what other people had done when facing this 'problem.' Each 'adult' shared their best intellectual thoughts and reasoning about young girls and pregnancy and Theresa's condition.

Joseph said, "My son was just doing what men are led to do by some kinds of girls."

Theresa jumped to her feet. "How dare you say that. You know nothing about the type of woman I am or the type of man he is." She pointed at Stephen who cowardly kept his eyes glued to the carpet. "I've listened to you all talk for the past hour like I'm not even here. I'm not a girl and this isn't a condition. I'm sorry that you think this is your problem, but it isn't, it's my problem and my decision."

She rushed out the front door, plopped down on the porch step, and forced herself to keep back the tears pushing to escape. Theresa had no answer either. What should she do?

A minute later, Stephen came out and sat down next to her. After a long pause, he spoke, but did not make eye contact. "I think you should go ahead with the abortion."

"Yeah, what your father wants," blurted out Theresa.

He didn't respond.

"I can't understand why you hate me," she said.

"I don't hate you."

She turned to face him. "We could be happy. We could find an apartment off campus—"

"You mean get married?"

"What's so awful about that?" asked Theresa. "Do you love me?" She waited but knew the response she ached to hear would not come. She remembered her mother asking the same of her father sixteen years earlier. The silence communicated everything.

Stephen pushed his hands through his hair still not meeting her eyes. "This is a problem for both of us. I don't see any other way out."

Numbness filled her body as she took from her pocket the torn piece of paper that Dr. Roberts had given her. "I don't have enough money to do it and pay for school, too."

He took the paper from her. "I'll pay for it."

Theresa sighed. "Make the arrangements, then. You can at least drive me there so I don't have to ride my bike."

They sat in silence.

CHAPTER 21
(2006)

Darcy and Liz sat captivated, unable to find words. They waited for Theresa to speak.

"Excuse me," Theresa said, and she went to the restroom and locked the door behind her. She walked to the sink and stared at herself in the mirror. She expected at some point those long-ago emotions would bubble up while sharing with the girls. It was hard, but important if not for them, for her.

Using warm water, she wet a paper towel and patted her face. Then she used the toilet, touched up her lipstick, and returned to the table where Darcy and Liz talked quietly to each other.

"Sorry," Theresa apologized as she slipped back into the booth.

"No, that's okay, Ms. Clavin," said Darcy.

"That guy was a real jerk," added Liz.

Theresa glanced at her watch. "Maybe that's enough for today."

The girls nodded, closed their laptops, and started putting things away.

"We want to find out what happened, Ms. Clavin," said Liz.

Theresa cocked her head. "So, you want to hear more?"

Darcy zipped up her backpack. "Yeah, we'll be back tomorrow after school."

"For sure," Liz added. "I think this paper will get us a good grade."

They bid Theresa goodbye and walked out of the coffee shop chattering to each other. Theresa was certainly sharing a lot more than they could put in their assignment. Yet, she hoped they might learn something from her experiences. Isn't that what 'old' people are supposed to do, pass on wisdom? She chuckled, exited, and lit her cigarette, swallowing a long, deep inhalation. The smoke spewed from her nostrils and mouth as she exhaled out all the emotions from the day. So many stories.

Liz drove by in her mother's mini-van and both girls waved.

Caught again. Theresa returned the wave.

The next afternoon, Theresa was happy to see Darcy and Liz arrive right on time. "You driving a little faster, today, Liz?"

Darcy laughed. "We just left earlier."

Liz rolled her eyes.

Theresa handed them a twenty and motioned to the front counter. "Go ahead and get your goodies. I've already got mine."

Darcy returned with the same drink as the day before. A huge cup with a chocolate stir and an oversized chocolate donut with one bite already taken.

"What is that?" Asked Theresa pointing at her mug wondering if perhaps she should branch out and try something new.

"Half hot chocolate and half coffee. I can't stand coffee straight."

"She's wimpy," said Liz as she sat down with her black coffee and a huge chunk of coffee cake. "But she loves chocolate more than boys."

"Shut up," responded Darcy playfully.

The girls settled in, opened up their laptops, and looked up at Theresa.

"You know," Theresa said, thinking about what they had witnessed her doing the day before in the coffee shop parking lot. "You young ladies should *never* start smoking. I picked up the habit at twenty-three. Please don't do it."

Darcy shook her head. "Of course not, Ms. Clavin."

Liz placed her fingers on her keyboard waiting to type. "Did you have the…um…?"

Theresa stirred her coffee. "Abortions were illegal in 1958. I had heard about girls hemorrhaging to death or getting seriously ill from terrible infections. There were stories about back alley rooms, dirty conditions, contaminated instruments, unlicensed doctors. I hoped none of it was true, but I honestly didn't know. I was very frightened."

CHAPTER 22
(1958)

Theresa sat unmoving in Stephen's car as he drove to the address given to him over the phone. She sensed his discomfort as he rambled but didn't try to put him at ease.

"So, how are your classes going?" he said.

"Fine," Theresa replied coldly.

"How are your teachers?"

"Fine."

There was a brief pause before his next question. "Do you know what courses you're taking next semester?"

"Stephen," said Theresa, exasperated.

"What?"

She shook her head at him. "You don't care anyway."

The remainder of the drive was silent, leaving her in a flurry of conflicting thoughts about the man she thought she loved, and the loss of any hope of having a life or family with him. She tried to force frightening images from her mind from the impending procedure. What might happen? Could she die?

Thirty minutes later, they turned down a road with several one-story buildings, each with two front doors. Stephen checked his paper, parked at the curb near the last duplex on the block, and handed Theresa an envelope. Inside she saw two hundred and fifty dollars in cash.

He pointed at the gray building. "Number nine. The one on the left."

Theresa looked at door number nine which had red paint peeling and a gash on the lower right side. She couldn't move; everything weighted down like lead.

"Well?" Stephen prompted.

She continued to stare at the door. Her heart thumped in her chest. After everything she had attempted, all the abuse she'd put her body through, that tiny life inside had not given up. It refused to let go. It was a fighter, like her.

Stephen consulted his watch and tapped his fingers on the steering wheel. "Theresa, go on. I'll wait here."

She suddenly snapped. "Take me to Jackie's."

"Why?"

"I can't do this. I'll have my baby even if I can't keep it."

Stephen shook his head, his voice firm. "That is not what we agreed to."

But she wanted nothing more to do with him and didn't care what he thought. She threw the money at him and yelled. "If this is your way of solving a problem, then I don't ever want to talk with you again…ever. Now, take me to Jackie's."

He hit the steering wheel with his hand and screeched his car into a U-turn. Within twenty minutes, he pulled into Jackie's driveway. Theresa got out of the car, walked to the front door, and knocked.

Jackie soon answered and Theresa immediately broke into tears, melting into the arms of her friend.

"Oh, honey," said Jackie, walking her inside.

Theresa never looked back at Stephen. At that moment, she hated him. She tried to catch her breath in between sobs. "I just couldn't do it."

Jackie helped her lay down in the back bedroom and tucked the covers up around her neck. "Thank God. We'll find another solution, all right?" Theresa nodded. "You get some sleep."

Emotional exhaustion overtook her and she slept for a long time.

When she awoke, she laid there taking in all the details of the nice, homey decor in the bedroom—bright yellow and rich purple bedspread, small paintings of landscapes on the wall, fresh pink carnations in a vase. A cool breeze blew into the room through the partially open window, causing the white curtains to billow softly. So peaceful. In a flash, Theresa knew in her heart what she must do.

CHAPTER 23
(2006)

"Even though I had considered keeping the baby, struggling to work and raise it on my own sounded impossible," Theresa told Darcy and Liz. "And in 1959, both the child and I would have been frowned upon and I didn't want that. So I returned to college, the house, and my classes. I didn't tell anyone else about my pregnancy. Too many people knew already."

"So, your dad and stepmother didn't find out?" asked Darcy.

Theresa shook her head. She could never allow that to happen. Never. "Towards my third month, I got sick at the slightest smell of food. I ate boxes of crackers, but they only helped provide me something to throw up."

Liz grimaced. "My mom has morning sickness. It looks awful, puking most of the time."

"It is rather awful," admitted Theresa. "Kathleen, my roommate, always tried convincing me to go out to the dances and movies and just to socialize, but I kept focused on my studies. She used to ask me how I got so boring."

Darcy typed a few more notes, then said, "Couldn't people tell you were pregnant?"

"I wore oversized clothes and a corset."

Liz looked up from her note-taking. "You wore a corset? Isn't that something from back in the seventeen hundreds or something?"

Theresa laughed. "It wasn't very comfortable, and I couldn't wait to take it off." She recalled nothing feeling more pleasant than freeing and scratching her expanding tummy. "I stayed at Jackie and Ben's house as often as I could. I didn't have to hide anything there and enjoyed sleeping for as long as I wanted."

"Your friend sounds really sweet," commented Darcy.

A smile donned Theresa's face. "A close friend is truly rare. Jackie didn't agree with all my decisions, still doesn't. But I can talk to her about anything and she's always there to hold on to."

Liz bumped her shoulder against Darcy, who grinned back at her.

Theresa had seen the girls together for years and hoped they would continue being close. Although, often once past high school, sometimes it became more of a challenge.

"So, what did Stephen do? Did he even acknowledge you anymore?" asked Liz.

"He called one night and asked if we could talk. I was pretty skeptical, but I agreed. He drove us out to the hills and we parked."

CHAPTER 24
(1958)

Stephen and Theresa sat in Stephen's car. He silently gazed out from the hillside to the city lights twinkling far below. She stared at the bright stars overhead.

"Theresa, I've been thinking." He rolled down his window and fresh air blew in. "Maybe we should get married."

Her head snapped towards him. Now he's saying this? Really? "Your father said if we got married he wouldn't pay for your schooling and you'd have to find a job."

"I know. I talked to him again, several times. He finally said he'd still pay for my school and let us live with them."

Theresa looked back out the window, she hadn't planned on this happening. Isn't this what she wanted just a few short months ago, to marry Stephen? To become a part of his family? To bear children with him? She thought about his father's offer to continue paying for his son's schooling. What about her education? What about her?

She noticed his clenched hands, waiting for her answer. Not sure if it was stubbornness, spitefulness, or sensibility, a wave of certainty hit her. She would remain in control of her own life. That would not be given up to anyone else. "No," she said.

"What do you mean?"

"No, I won't marry you."

He wrinkled his forehead. "I thought that's what you wanted?"

"What I need is twenty-five dollars for maternity clothes. Then I'll never ask you for anything ever again."

"But—"

"Stephen, you don't love me," Theresa explained, calmly. "You don't love your own child. So, how can you think this would work? No, you can't have either of us."

Stephen didn't try to change her mind.

Theresa periodically spent time with William to keep up appearances to other classmates that she was dating. Two weeks before the end of the school semester, he walked her back to the dormitory. She did not go in, instead remained staring at the ground.

"Are you all right?"

"I'm pregnant."

His eyes opened wide then fell into a frown. "Uh, it's obviously not mine."

She snickered. "Of course not."

"Who's the father?"

Theresa paused. "Stephen."

Clenching his jaw, William shook his head. "What does he think about it?"

"He doesn't love me. Never did."

"He's a loser. You were so 'in love,' you never even saw that he used you."

Theresa turned to him. "So, why didn't you say something?"

"Would you have believed me?"

She stroked her growing belly for a few moments. "I was so naïve."

William placed his hand on her shoulder. "What are you going to do?"

"Give it up for adoption."

"Really? You aren't going to keep it?"

"This baby deserves two parents. Ones that can provide a stable home and love for it. Love is all I can give, and for my child, that's not enough."

William sighed, and she sensed his hurt feelings. "I'm not talking about your daughter," she clarified. "You're still a part of her life."

He didn't respond.

"Right?"

William nodded. "Right."

"After our final tests, I'm going to Los Angeles to find a home for pregnant girls, have the baby, give it up for adoption, then return to finish my last semester of school."

"Los Angeles by yourself? I don't—"

She took hold of both his hands and squeezed them. "I'll be alright, William. Don't worry."

"How can you say that?"

"Thank you for being a good friend to me. Between you and Jackie..." Theresa teared up, leaned forward, and kissed his cheek.

A smirk grew on his face.

CHAPTER 25
(1959)

Theresa stood before the first maternity home. It was located in the midst of a residential neighborhood somewhere in Los Angeles. A ripped curtain in the family room window clung to the rod, and all the others were drawn tightly shut. A few shingles had come loose, and the yard consisted of overgrown weeds.

She wasn't liking the appearance of this place. Theresa inhaled and approached the front door that displayed an 'Enter' sign. She pushed it open and stepped into a rather dingy entry.

A girl of about sixteen emerged from a bathroom and pointed down the hallway. "Last door on the left."

"Thanks."

The girl walked away saying nothing further, and Theresa glanced into the restroom. Water was splashed on the mirrors and the counter, and the toilet needed scrubbing.

The next room held four pregnant teenagers talking loudly and using language that would have won Theresa a mouthful of soap by Dorothy. A couple of them glared at her, and one closed the door in her face.

As she made her way down the shadowy hall, she saw another young resident crying on her bed. Theresa's insides churned. The thought of living in these conditions for the next few months repulsed her. Maybe she should go somewhere else.

"In here," came a curt voice from behind her.

Turning, Theresa saw a tall, thin woman in her fifties chomping on gum, her hair styled short and dyed red. She led Theresa into a small office where they both sat down at an old desk.

"I'm Abigail."

"Theresa."

Abigail skipped any niceties, her tone flat. "When are you due?" Theresa imagined she'd asked that question hundreds of times before and this time held no difference to her.

"In June. So how exactly does this work?"

The woman shuffled through papers as she spoke. "You stay here until it comes time. You go to the hospital, are sedated, and have the kid. Then, it's handed over to the appropriate people. That's it. You're done."

Theresa frowned. "You make it sound so, so…"

Abigail raised her head and shrugged. "So what?"

Unable to come up with a descriptive enough word, Theresa continued. "I'd be able to see the baby first, right?"

"No, you'll be asleep."

Theresa had considered that many times over the previous few months, but she remained adamant. "Well, I would want to see my baby."

"That is out of the question."

Theresa remained firm. "But, I want to be sure he or she is okay."

A girl with a very large stomach waddled to the doorway and the woman waved her away. "We don't operate that way."

Frustrated at her insensitivity, Theresa rose. She would get her way. "Well, I guess this home won't work then."

"I guess not," said Abigail as if she couldn't care less. She focused on her paperwork.

Theresa walked out of the facility. What a horrid place and horrible woman.

The second home was in a nicer area and had no visible maintenance issues. Some of the girls sat on the porch swing, joking with each other. Theresa entered the home.

A woman in her sixties grasped Theresa's hands warmly. "Hello there. I'm Delores."

At once, Theresa felt better. "I'm Theresa."

"Why don't we go have a chat," Delores invited, and they went into a nicely decorated, roomy office with a fireplace. "Would you like something to drink? Perhaps some hot tea?"

"No. I'm fine. Thank you."

Delores smiled. "Are you looking for a place to stay for a bit?"

Theresa nodded. "The girls here seem happy."

"We try to keep a relaxed atmosphere because the young ladies are already under so much stress."

"It is a difficult situation," said Theresa. Yes, this seemed like a good place. "Even though I'm going forward with the adoption, I would like to see the baby before giving it up."

Delores's smile faded and she shook her head. "Oh dear, that wouldn't be how it would work."

"Why not?"

"Because you'd be put under."

Theresa's shoulders fell as the disappointment registered.

"I know after nine months, you must be curious. But, why would you take the chance of getting attached?"

Theresa had thought of that possibility. "I just have to."

The woman apologized. "I'm sorry. I wish you luck trying to find a place that would permit that."

Theresa paused, staring at a family photo on the desk.

Delores noticed and beamed proudly. "My adopted daughter and two grandsons."

Forcing a smile, Theresa asked. "Would there be a way to make sure that the people adopting would love and provide everything for my baby?"

Delores came around and sat in the chair next to Theresa. "My dear. We do our best to ensure our adoptive parents meet certain criteria, but no one can guarantee what you're asking."

Theresa sighed, then looked up at Delores. "I'll think about it." She left, willing herself to remain positive about the visit to the final home.

Standing in the kitchen of the third maternity house, the woman shook her head. "I'm sorry, but we only take girls under twenty-one here. No exceptions. Besides, seeing the baby after the birth is not allowed."

Theresa traveled across town on another bus, and walked into a hotel lobby that looked just as rundown and tired as she felt. She had stayed there many years earlier, but the property no longer had the appeal it once did. The clerk said he only had a room on the fifth floor and she accepted it thinking only of getting her shoes off. Theresa saw a discarded newspaper tossed in a trash bin and fished it out. She walked to the elevator only to see black tape covering the buttons indicating it wasn't working. Couldn't anything go her way that day?

After catching her breath from climbing five flights of stairs, she called Jackie to report in about the disappointments of the day.

"Are you coming back?" asked Jackie.

"No. I'm not whipped yet. I've never had a problem getting work so I'll just find a job and pay for my own expenses."

"You could do that here."

"I can't," Theresa said desiring the privacy that being around strangers would bring.

Jackie sighed. "Alright. Well be sure to call me tomorrow and let me know how things go."

After their goodbyes, Theresa found the Help Wanted ads and spread the newspaper out on her bed. She spent over an hour reading and circling potential employers. When she could no longer keep her eyes open, she turned off the light and fell into a deep sleep.

CHAPTER 26
(1959)

The next morning, Theresa put on a blue maternity dress, clipped back her hair, brushed on a little mascara and a hint of lipstick. Inspecting herself in the mirror, she smiled at how presentable she looked despite her bulging tummy. She would find a job today. Who wouldn't hire her with all her work experience? Off went the lights and she walked confidently from the hotel door.

The first employer she tried was Western Union. Having worked for that company while going to community college, she believed it would be easy to get rehired. Theresa had always been a dedicated worker having missed very few days and never being tardy. She filled out the paperwork and handed it to the personnel clerk.

"Wait here," said a small-framed woman in her early twenties before disappearing through a door.

Thirty minutes passed before Theresa was led into the office of an elderly man—not the same one who had hired her before. "Have a seat," he said as he skimmed her application.

The chair was hard and small for her expanding body, so she balanced on the front edge. "Thank you for seeing me."

The man set down the paper and raised his eyes. They went straight to her stomach. "You want a job. And you're expecting?"

Theresa nodded. "Yes sir. I'm a previous employee for Western Union and—"

"I can see that on your application," he interrupted. "Unfortunately, we're not hiring at this time."

She frowned. "But, you had an ad in the newspaper for telegraph operators."

"I'm sorry but those positions have been filled. Perhaps check back in a few months, after you have the baby."

"Just because I'm pregnant doesn't mean I can't work. I've already been trained—"

The man stood. "I said the positions are filled."

He was a lousy liar. How unfair. She left the building realizing her plan might be harder to implement than she originally thought.

All day, Theresa plodded into office buildings, retail stores, and insurance companies. People's responses varied from sincere apologies to skeptical comments about her being capable of performing. Back in her hotel late that afternoon, she sat on her bed rubbing her swollen and achy feet. Tomorrow was another day. She'd try again because what else could she do?

Day three in Los Angeles was spent on her ongoing job search at more potential employers—drug stores, a book store, and even a shoe merchant where the salesman tried to sell her some more comfortable leather shoes. If only she had the money. When he kept pressing and began describing their generous layaway plan, Theresa got up and left.

Everywhere, Theresa received rejections. Some people pleasant and others not. Regardless, none of them appeared interested in hiring a woman who was six months with child.

In her room, Theresa counted her remaining money. A meager amount, not enough to last long. She picked up the phone, but after some consideration, she hung it back up not wanting to call Jackie with failure. First, she must succeed. Despite being exhausted, the worried thoughts in her mind kept swirling, preventing her from resting much at all.

The fourth day resulted as the other days, no luck, no interest, no, no, no. The only thing she had to show for her efforts were two bleeding blisters on her heels.

During her hobble back to her hotel, a winter storm rolled in dropping the temperature into the forties. Theresa wrapped her coat around herself as darkness came quickly. She decided to try one last place—the diner across from the hotel. After entering, she loosened her coat and savored the aroma of simmering pot roast and pungent coffee.

A waitress carrying a full tray of food above her head stopped. "Table for one?"

If only she could afford to sit down and enjoy a hot meal. "Actually, I'm looking for a job. Do you have anything?"

"I'm sorry, hun. Nothing's available." The waitress rolled her eyes. "In fact, the new manager's looking to fire a few people. I don't know how they expect us to—"

Theresa turned away and returned to the outside cold.

Rain was falling and the streets were growing deserted except for the last few people hurrying home with umbrellas, and a couple of homeless men drinking while huddled around a trashcan fire to ward off the chill.

The elevator was still in need of repair, so again, Theresa climbed the steps up to her room. Out of breath, she shut her door, leaned her head against it, and cried. She had tried everything and nothing was working. There was no way out.

She wiped her runny nose on the rough, wet sleeve of her coat. The steaming window caught her attention and she slowly walked over, unlatched it, and struggled to push it open. It unstuck with a clunk and she slid the frame upward.

Theresa looked at the twelve-inch window sill for a moment before lifting first one leg, then the other to perch herself on the damp wood. With feet dangling high above the dark, dirty alley, she closed her eyes. Raindrops wet her face and she shivered.

Once again she was eleven years old on the day her mother had died. Theresa inched further out on the window ledge as she had stepped forward to the edge of that jagged cliff. There was no one to come sweep her off her feet as Carl had done. She'd die in childbirth like her Momma. Her child would have no one, no mother, just like her. She couldn't imagine putting her child through a life devoid of love, as she had experienced for so much of her own. With the rain soaked through to her skin, Theresa opened her eyes and stared at the water droplets cascading towards the asphalt below. Ending it all would be the best thing for both of them.

Theresa let her eyes close again and moved closer to the action that would solve everything. No more pain, no more problem. That would be easier for everyone. A whisper fell from her lips. "God forgive me. Momma, I'm coming home."

Suddenly, there was a loud knock at the door.

Theresa jumped as her eyes shot open. One shoe tumbled to the ground as she grabbed the window frame to regain her balance. She sat frozen trying to ignore the pounding. Who could that be? Who would that be? Probably someone at the wrong room.

The person outside would not cease, so Theresa finally crawled back into the room—wet and cold. Unable to stop trembling, she shuffled to the door and called out with a weakened voice, "Who's there?"

"It's William."

William? How could that be? Theresa flung open the door and stared at him in disbelief.

"Theresa, you're all wet. Are you all right?"

Unable to process anything more, she melted into tears and he stepped closer to catch her from falling. Theresa cried in his embrace for a long while. He felt so safe, so warm, so reassuring. After regaining a little composure, she pushed back slightly. "What are you doing here? How did you find me?"

"When Jackie didn't hear anything for three days, she asked if I'd come check on you."

Theresa managed a soggy smile at the mention of her dear friend's name.

"You know, you do have people who care about you," he said.

She began sobbing again and William held her close, patting her back. "Come on, I'll take you home."

Together, they gathered her few possessions and secured them in her suitcase. With his arm around her, William helped her downstairs, paid for the hotel bill, and settled her into the passenger seat of his car.

For ninety minutes he and Theresa did not speak. William honored her need for silence as she alternated between crying and having no tears left to shed.

As they walked up to Jackie and Ben's door, it opened and there stood Jackie in a yellow dressing gown. Seeing Theresa's red eyes and puffy face, she encircled her younger friend and pulled her into a hug.

This triggered the return of Theresa's tears, but now they fell from relief and from the reality that she felt loved. She was lovable.

William set Theresa's suitcase in the hallway as Jackie brought Theresa into the house and toward the now familiar guest room. She helped Theresa with a nightgown and into bed, once again tucking the blanket under her chin.

Theresa stared at her friend. "I don't know what I'm going to —"

"We'll figure it out. Get some sleep, now."

CHAPTER 27
(2006)

Darcy and Liz sat frozen, staring at Theresa, who tried to sip coffee from her empty cup.

"Jackie had saved the day for the umpteenth time," Theresa said.

Liz blinked her watery eyes. "For sure."

"It was a hard time and I still had to figure out what to do."

"Geez, I can't imagine," said Darcy.

Theresa arched her eyebrows. "Hopefully, neither of you will ever be in that position."

The girls sighed, eyes big, no words.

"Not everyone will care what happens to you," said Theresa. "But, someone will. You just can't give up like I almost did."

Darcy rubbed her forehead. "That kid sure must have wanted to live."

"Thankfully, God didn't give up either," added Theresa.

"What happened next?" asked Liz.

"I stayed with Jackie and Ben for a few days, doing lots of thinking and sleeping and more thinking. Then, Ben came home with some interesting news."

CHAPTER 28
(1959)

The light in Jackie's kitchen shifted from shadows to brightness and back again as numerous fluffy, white clouds journeyed past the sun. Showers fell on and off all day long and the air remained chilly. Theresa and Jackie sat quietly at the table drinking hot tea.

Ben came in the front door and walked directly to the kitchen. Theresa didn't hear the clatter of him dropping his car keys in the silver container on the hall table as he did routinely after arriving home every day.

Jackie stood and greeted him with a hug. "Hey, honey. How was your day?"

"Interesting," he said as he kissed his wife's cheek. "Hello, Theresa."

"Hi, Ben."

He looked at Jackie. "I need to talk with you."

Jackie nodded. "Sure."

They disappeared into their bedroom, leaving Theresa to mull over how long she should stay at her friend's home. She certainly didn't want to cause difficulties with Ben. Perhaps he was getting tired of having her moping around with no end in sight.

The couple re-emerged and sat down.

Jackie reached across the table and gave Theresa's hand a squeeze. "We might have a solution."

Theresa straightened up.

"Do you think you'd consider a private adoption?" asked Ben.

"Um, maybe?"

"I was talking to a man at work, today. He happened to mention that he and his wife want to adopt."

Theresa's heart sped a little. "Do you know anything about them?"

"Not about the wife, and I've only worked with him for a few months. He seems to be a decent guy. Never misses work and people like him."

"Why are they looking at adoption?"

"They can't have children."

Theresa sat back in her chair to ponder the possibility. It didn't take long. "I'd like to hear more."

Ben got up from the table. "Alright, I'll tell him."

After an anxious night and day, Theresa waited for Ben to arrive home from work. Before he even closed the door, she was on her feet asking. "What'd he say?"

He handed her a piece of paper with a name and phone number written on it. "This is his attorney. You need to set up a time to meet with him."

She embraced him. "Thanks, Ben. I'll call him first thing in the morning."

The next evening, Theresa stood at the front door of Gus Hanten, attorney-at-law.

She wondered why her instructions were to come to his home and not to go to his office location. Also odd was that his secretary insisted they schedule a night meeting. Yet, his school-aged children were visible through the window playing a game of Scrabble, so Theresa relaxed a little and rang the doorbell. Her hopes raised high for the outcome.

The door opened to a tall man in his fifties dressed in a brown suit with a loosened tie.

"Mr. Hanten?"

"You must be Theresa. Come in." He motioned her into a small home office.

She sat on an over-stuffed couch while he stood by his desk, looking down at her. "My secretary told me you're interested in giving your child up for adoption."

Theresa nodded.

Hanten eased into a squeaky office chair. "Thanks for coming to the house. These types of situations can be a bit tricky sometimes."

"Why is that?"

He removed a file from a drawer. "This is considered gray-market. I don't handle those at the office."

"What do you mean, gray-market?"

Gus Hanten folded his hands. His chair groaned when he leaned back. "As the biological mother, you can take as much time as you want to give up the child."

Theresa bit her lip. Chances are good for seeing the baby after the birth.

"If you decide to go through with the adoption, you've got six months to change your mind and reclaim the baby."

How badly the couple must want this child Theresa considered. "That must be hard for the adopting parents."

"It is risky for them as they retain no legal rights or recourse. But, these folks are willing to take it."

"What can you tell me about them?"

The attorney shrugged. "Very stable. Appear to be responsible and financially able to provide more than adequately for a family. They own a home and a car and the husband holds down a steady job."

Her second concern answered, at least as best as she could tell.

"I think they're perfectly suited to raise another child."

"Oh, they already have one?"

"Yes, they adopted a boy last year."

A sibling already in place. Her baby would not be an only child. "Would I meet the parents?"

Hanten shook his head. "No. I'd make all the appropriate arrangements."

Theresa honestly wasn't sure she'd even want to meet the couple. That might complicate things. She asked a few more questions and then explained to Hanten how she had one semester remaining in college before earning her bachelor's degree in elementary education. She hoped that would impress him. But then again, maybe he didn't really care. "I'll be returning to finish school after the birth."

He nodded.

"Mr. Hanten. I am not going to change my mind about giving up my child. The only decision left is who will receive the baby."

"My client has made a considerable offer."

Theresa winced. She couldn't possibly *sell* her baby.

She shook her head. "No, I don't want any money. I can work and pay for my own bills, even though I'm having a hard time finding a job in this condition." She smiled and pointed to her belly. "I'll keep trying though."

Hanten scratched his chin. "There isn't any pressure here, Theresa. Why don't you think about it? In the meantime, I'll call my clients to let them know you're considering them."

Theresa laid in bed that night, thinking she'd gotten that far, now she must figure out the rest. She had already convinced herself this couple was her best option. But the worry of still trying to secure work prevented her from sleeping much.

In the morning, she called and told Mr. Hanten that the couple would receive her child when it was born. "I only have one request. I want to see and hold my baby."

"Shouldn't be a problem."

A sense of relief melted through Theresa. Finally, she had what she wanted and it didn't seem to be an issue at all.

"Come by the house on Thursday evening at seven and we'll square things up," invited Hanten.

Hanten appeared pleased when he greeted Theresa at her next appointment. "After you called, I spoke with my clients, and though you are not to know the adoptive parents, as I stated before, an unusual opportunity is being offered to you."

"What is it?"

"The man has an older brother who's divorced and lives alone. He's agreed to allow you to stay with him for free in exchange for cooking and housekeeping. The adopting parents will pay all your medical expenses."

Theresa began liking the couple more and felt a little jump inside her belly. She accepted it as the baby offering his or her approval. "That's extremely generous."

"If you accept this arrangement, you are to respect that you will not push to get to know the adoptive parents."

"Of course not," she agreed, yet hoping this would afford her a chance to learn more about the couple.

Hanten continued. "You'll keep complete control over your child until you choose to give it over to them."

Even though Theresa promised she would give these parents her baby, they had no guarantee that she would actually follow through. They were taking a huge chance on someone they'd never met before and never would. They had no idea what kind of person she was. She nodded at Hanten. "Please, thank the couple and tell them I will accept their offer."

CHAPTER 29
(1959)

A week later, Theresa stood on the porch of Phil Gerhart, an older brother of the soon-to-be father of her child and her child's future uncle. She stared at the front door wondering what to expect. Holding her breath, she rang the doorbell.

The door opened to a man in his late fifties. His hair was receding and graying and he pushed black-framed glasses higher on his nose. The lenses so thick, they made his eyes appear larger than normal. "You Theresa?"

"Yes, are you Mr. Gerhart?"

"I am," he said with a warm smile. He immediately took her suitcase from her hand and opened the door allowing her to come inside. "I'll show you your bedroom."

"Thanks." She followed him to a small room.

He fumbled for the light. "I might as well tell you now, I don't see very well in the dark." He finally found the switch.

She looked around the room liking that it wasn't fancy, but homey. There were two mismatched pillows on the bed and the edges of the faded green bedspread hung longer on one side than the other. A gold-painted crucifix was mounted on the wall above the dresser. The room held a good feel.

He placed the suitcase on the bed. "I hope this works."

"This is wonderful. Thank you very much, Mr. Gerhart."

"Call me Phil."

She nodded. The awkward silence crawled by as Theresa perused the room for a third time.

Phil gave a sheepish grin and asked, "So, what's for dinner?"

She laughed. "What do you like?"

"Anything you want to make would be appreciated. I'm sick of my lousy cooking. Everything tastes like salted cardboard."

"Well, let's go see what you've got then," she said and he turned and led her to the kitchen.

Dirty dishes sat in the sink and the counters needed wiping down. There was a hole in the window curtain, and clothes piled high in a laundry basket begged to be folded.

He noticed her taking everything in. "I definitely could use some help around here."

Theresa raised her palms in jest. "That's me."

The refrigerator held not much beyond some leftover meatloaf on a plate, two wrinkled oranges, a small glass container of milk, and the typical everyday condiments.

"You have any bread?" she asked.

Phil nodded and opened a cupboard with a partial loaf of white bread, and two open boxes of corn flakes.

"Tell you what," Theresa said. "How about a sandwich tonight, then tomorrow we can go to the market and buy some groceries?"

He pointed his index finger. "Fine idea."

She removed the meatloaf and gave it a sniff. It didn't smell bad. A few minutes later, she put the meatloaf sandwich in front of Phil who sat patiently at the table.

He noticed only one sandwich. "Aren't you hungry?"

Theresa shook her head preferring to wait for something a bit more appetizing.

"See, even you refuse to eat my cooking and we just met."

She laughed.

"Well, at least sit down and keep me company," Phil said.

She sat down across from him as he took his first bite.

He grinned. "Mmmmm. Why do sandwiches always taste better when someone else makes them?"

Theresa chuckled. Phil came across to her as a friendly, down-to-earth man, and she liked his sense of humor. This situation was far better than being held up in one of those maternity homes. She desperately wanted to ask about his brother and sister-in-law, although she was unsure exactly how to begin. Perhaps his brother had instructed him not to reveal anything. Theresa certainly wasn't going to attempt to meet the adoptive parents, she just hoped to find out more about them.

"Mr. Gerhart—"

He cocked his head and arched his eyebrows.

She smiled. "I mean, Phil. Obviously, I'm aware of your brother. Do you have other siblings?"

"There are eight of us," he said and took another bite.

"Quite a handful for your parents."

"Mmm hmm."

"Where do you fall in the line? Youngest? Oldest? Somewhere in between?"

"I'm on the older side of things. Edward's the baby of the family."

She waited for him to elaborate.

He shook his head. "The baby at forty. Hard to believe how fast time goes."

Theresa nodded in agreement even though her past several months seemed to have dragged by.

"Edward's the one that went to Gus Hanten for help."

"Oh," she said. After a hesitation, she took the chance. "I know I'll never meet your brother, but what's he like?"

Phil wiped his mouth, got up, and left the kitchen.

She wasn't sure what to think about his abrupt exit. Did she say something wrong? Maybe she shouldn't have asked so soon. Theresa sat motionless, waiting, hoping for his return.

Soon he reemerged carrying a framed photograph. "This is Edward and his wife, Catherine." He held out the frame until she accepted it. She bit her lip and examined the picture of the couple who would be her child's parents.

Edward was a big man, at least six foot two or three. His hair was thinning but hadn't begun to turn gray yet. He had his arm encircled around the waist of his shorter wife. She wore a well-fitted dress showing off her petite figure. A clip held back her dark hair and her brown eyes sparkled. Theresa lightly brushed her fingers over Catherine's beautiful smile. They looked happy.

She handed the frame back to Phil. "What a lovely couple."

Ben laid the photo on the table and sat back down.

"Edward's been working since he was a kid," said Phil. "When he was nine or ten, he was setting pins down at the bowling alley, and at thirteen, he caddied on the golf course. He gave every dime he made to our mother. Even spent a few years in the Marine Corps. Now he's a manager at a paper products company. He's always been a good provider for Catherine."

"How long have they been married?"

"Oh golly, let me think." Phil furrowed his brow. "It was the year World War II ended, so forty-five. I think…yeah, it was just before Christmas."

Theresa already calculated in her head. "Going on fourteen years."

"They tried for a long time for kids but it just didn't work out."

She focused on the dusty baseboards. Here she was dealing with her pregnancy like it's a problem, while poor Catherine wanted to get pregnant and never could.

Phil broke her silence. "Catherine's an excellent cook. I love eating at their house. She worked at the shredded wheat factory up until they adopted Robby last year."

"She'll soon be busy with two babies."

Phil shook his head. "No, not a baby. Robby's five now." He opened his wallet and pulled out another photograph. A little boy with black spiked hair offered the camera a tentative smile.

"They went to an orphanage wanting to adopt. Crazy story about that whole thing."

"What happened?"

"Well, when the people there brought in little Robby, they explained he'd been there for almost two years. Apparently, his mother gave him to the orphanage when he was three. Damndest thing was she kept his older and younger brothers."

Theresa tried to process how hard it must have been for a three-year-old to understand being forced to leave his home and family, all that he'd ever known. "How horrible." Then her own past popped into her thoughts. Dorothy certainly wasn't a decent mother by any stretch of the imagination. Perhaps it was best for Robby after all. At least he's with parents that want him now.

Phil finished his sandwich and ran a napkin across his mouth as Theresa awaited the rest of the story. "Those orphanage people warned my brother that they'd probably want to bring Robby back after the trial day was over and they assured him that would be alright."

Theresa grimaced.

"Supposedly, he could be quite the little devil. By the end of several trials, all the potential parents had returned him—like he was a library book."

She stared at him trying to fathom what repeated rejection might feel like for such a young child. Thankfully, she had her Momma during those crucial first years.

"Anyway, they brought Robby home. Catherine took him straight into the back bedroom, told him it was now his, and that he would never be going back to the orphanage."

Theresa felt a warmth develop in her chest and she couldn't conceal her smile. Edward and Catherine indeed must be caring parents to make a choice like that before spending any time with this little boy. Her admiration continued to increase for this couple.

"That's the type of mother Catherine is," Phil said. "I know she'll raise your baby..." Theresa's head dropped and Phil suddenly stopped his sentence. He rubbed his face. "I'm sorry, Theresa. I didn't mean—"

"No, no." She looked back at him. "I want to learn as much about them as you can tell me. My baby must have a good home with two loving parents."

Phil patted her hand. "We'll have plenty of time to talk. But, I'm tired. Got to get up early for work."

She started to gather up his empty plate and glass. "Of course. I'm sorry for asking so many questions."

"You can ask me anything."

"Thank you," she said.

Phil rose to leave the room. "Thanks for the sandwich. Goodnight, Theresa."

"Goodnight, Phil."

Twenty minutes later, Theresa stood staring at her bare body in front of the bathroom mirror. She couldn't help but smile in amusement at how her stretching stomach was pushing her belly button out.

Before crawling into bed, she got down on her knees and clasped her hands together like she used to do with Momma every night. She had almost given up on believing that God was even listening to her, but now perhaps she had His ear.

"Thank you, God, for Jackie, Ben, and William. And for Phil. Thank you for this couple who wants to adopt my baby, especially Catherine. I know you've chosen her to be the mother of my child. Please keep my baby safe. Amen."

Theresa climbed into bed, switched off the light, and snuggled underneath the lopsided green bedspread.

CHAPTER 30
(2006)

The air temperature in the coffee shop dropped so Theresa slipped on her sweater. "My three months at his home was a welcomed respite. I handled all the laundry and cleaning, which he genuinely appreciated. But, he also gave me the freedom to read, and I wrote about my feelings, my emotions, what was happening inside my body—that little life growing. And, I watched soap operas and game shows."

Liz pumped her fist. "Oh yeah."

They all laughed.

"I'd make Phil breakfast before he left for work, then go back to bed for a couple hours. I was so tired. I worked on my cooking skills and figured out how to make more than just potatoes. He thanked me after every meal I cooked."

"What a nice guy," said Darcy.

Theresa nodded. "He was truly honest and kind. Everything felt very natural. Many nights we would just sit and talk. Phil was a fascinating storyteller."

Liz tucked her legs under her body. "What did you talk about?"

"Oh goodness, everything. We talked about our pasts and futures and he answered every one of my questions about

Edward and Catherine. He took me to my doctor's appointments. He was like a father to me, one that I had longed for but never had. I was happy for the most part."

Darcy sighed. "That's so cool after everything."

"Of course, Phil knew I was going to give the baby up, but he only questioned me one time."

CHAPTER 31
(1959)

Two weeks before her due date, Theresa stood at the sink washing the supper dishes, tears running down her face. The past few days had become more bitter and sad. Her longing to keep the little life she had nurtured for the previous almost nine months had grown stronger. This baby had meant the beginning of a family for her. She thought of how she'd miss hearing the baby's first words, watching those staggering first steps, being able to comfort him or her on the first day of school. Theresa wouldn't teach this little human about life, share in his or her joys and anguish. Never would she feel the pride as her child accepted a college diploma, fell in love, got married, and had children—her grandchildren. She would miss it all.

Phil entered and she tried to sniff back her emotions, but he sensed her distress.

He walked up behind her and gently placed his arm around her shoulder. "Theresa, what's wrong?"

Unsure how to put into words the anguish bubbling inside of her, she did not answer.

Taking her by the shoulders, he turned her around until she faced him. He brushed the salty drops from her cheeks. "You're strong enough to raise this child yourself. You could change your mind."

Surprised by his statement, Theresa instantly stopped crying. "This child is not mine to keep."

"But—"

"No. I'm only the receptacle to carry and love it while it's in my body."

Phil looked to the floor.

"Someday, God will see that I have children that will have two parents."

He nodded and went to his bedroom.

Theresa paused, then walked to his room where she almost knocked but stopped instead, placing her ear against the closed door. When she heard Phil's own quiet sobs, she hurt to the core. Her eyes welled once more and she hurried away.

The next morning, Phil entered the kitchen as she was frying bacon. Theresa tried to act as she had so many other days but the air was heavy. "Good morning."

"Morning," he responded, sitting down at the table.

She served him his breakfast and went to pack his lunch for the day. Neither of them spoke further until he finished his scrambled eggs.

He rose and carried his empty plate to the counter. "Thank you."

Theresa turned to him. "I want you to take me to town today. Can you do that?"

He nodded.

After he arrived home from work, he drove Theresa downtown and parked by several small shops.

"Wait here," she said. She pushed the door open and stood up with some difficulty, attempting to maneuver the additional forty pounds of her pregnancy.

"Are you sure?"

She left him waiting as she disappeared into a local jewelry store. Ten minutes later, she reemerged carrying a blue paper bag. Once back in the car, she removed a small baggie, opened it, and into his hand poured out its contents—a tiny gold cross necklace.

"Will you be sure that my baby gets this?" she asked.

The little cross draped over his large fingers. "Of course."

"It will be a gift signifying my love for him or her, but more than my love—God's love." Theresa began to weep, and Phil comforted her like a heartbroken daughter.

That evening, Theresa waddled over to present Phil with what proved to be his favorite meal. He looked delighted as she sat down next to him.

"This is amazing," she said.

"I love your fried chicken."

"Ha. No, this." After shifting around a bit in her chair, the familiar rhythmic pulsing from the baby became more pronounced. She reached out to Phil's hand and rested it on the left side of her rounded tummy.

He gave a puzzled frown.

"Hiccups," she said, and they both smiled. After a minute Theresa got to her feet. "That's enough, now."

"How do you stop it? Stand on your head?"

She laughed. "The only thing that works is taking a shower. I'll see you tomorrow."

"Goodnight."

Theresa leaned against the tiled wall with her eyes shut as the warm water cascaded over her stomach. Eventually, the baby's hiccups ceased. As she lay down in bed and put her hands on her belly, the baby pushed its foot against her rib. She moved trying to relieve the pressure and the baby rolled over causing ripples to appear across her skin. She couldn't help but grin. This was the best part of carrying a child.

The next day, Theresa opened the door to a familiar face.

Her friend's mouth dropped open as she gaped at Theresa's belly. "You're as big as a house."

Theresa hugged her. "Hello, Alice."

Alice followed Theresa down the hall and into the kitchen. Phil swallowed the last bite of his meal.

"Phil, this is Alice, my friend from school."

"You're the infamous, Phil," said Alice.

He stood and shook her hand. "I appreciate you coming. I'm afraid if something happened after dark, I wouldn't be able to drive Theresa to the hospital. My vision's terrible at night."

"Glad to help save the day." Alice winked at Theresa. "We have a lot to catch up on, anyway."

"Well, I'm off to bed. You two visit."

They all said goodnight.

The following day, the two women chatted as Theresa attempted to hang Phil's laundered shirts on the clothesline. After a while, Alice got to her feet. "Let me do that. I don't need to see you sprawled out on the grass."

Theresa didn't argue and squeezed onto a patio chair. She rubbed the pain in the small of her back.

"Good thing you got to stay here," Alice said. "And, for free."

"I'm going to miss him. He's been like a father to me and he's told me so much about his brother and his wife. They sound like the perfect couple for this little one."

Another shirt was hung. "Why did Phil get divorced? He seems like a good man. Did he tell you what…"

Theresa held her head in her hands. Tears trickled down her face. Alice walked over and rubbed her friend's back.

"This is the hardest thing I've ever done. I wish I never—"

Alice put her fingers to Theresa's lips. "God gave you the courage badge. You gotta wear it."

Theresa inhaled a long, deep breath.

"Let me finish up out here. You go lay down."

With a nod, Theresa wobbled back to the house.

Eight days past Theresa's due date, Alice put down a plate of pork chops on the table. Phil shook out his napkin. Theresa hadn't slept much and picked at her food.

After dinner, the women remained at the table playing cards. Rummy was the game that evening, but Theresa continued to squirm in her seat.

"You got ants in your pants?" asked Alice.

"I can't get comfortable. I think I'll just go to bed."

"Fine. I'm worn out anyway after doing all your housework, today," Alice chided.

Theresa gave a slight smile and shuffled to her bedroom. She slowly got into her night clothes and awkwardly climbed in between the sheets. With a groan, she reached out and pulled the string on the bedside lamp and struggled to find a satisfying position that seemed impossible. Lying on one side, she finally relaxed. Ten seconds later, her eyes shot open as she felt a popping sensation, followed by a gush of warm water between her legs. She turned the light back on. Pushing herself up, she dangled her swollen feet over the side of the bed and looked at her soaked gown.

"Oh boy," she said aloud. "This is it." The experience of childbirth would be one more challenge she must face alone. She wished her mother was with her and a memory rushed into

Theresa's head. The day that her mother stared right into her nine-year-old daughter's eyes and said, "Today will be scary for you, but you are to grow up even more." Theresa forced out the thoughts about her mother dying during the birth of her second child. There was no stopping what would come now.

"Alice?" Theresa called out. "Alice?"

Alice ran into the room. "You got another chore for me?"

Theresa sat stiffly. "My water just broke."

Her friend took charge. "Well then, we've got to go." She removed a partially pre-packed suitcase from under the bed, opened it, and started packing the rest of Theresa's clothes and bathroom items. Theresa pulled on an oversized maternity dress and slipped on sandals as she chattered nervously.

Dressed in pajamas and a robe, Phil showed up in the doorway. "Everything alright?"

"The kids decided to make an appearance," said Alice.

He stepped back.

Alice snapped the latches on the suitcase and hustled out of the room with it as Phil walked with Theresa to the front door.

She threw her arms around him. "You've been so kind to me."

He held her in the hug. "You're the strongest person I know."

"Please Phil, watch out for my baby. Please make sure it's loved."

He nodded. "I promise I'll be there. I love you, sweetheart, be careful."

"I love you too, Phil. I will never forget you."

They smiled at each other, both fighting back tears.

Alice yelled out. "Come on. You want to have that baby right here?"

Theresa gave a nervous laugh and she walked to the car.

"See ya', Phil," said Alice.

Theresa waved to Phil, sorry to say goodbye. Then, she experienced her first contraction.

CHAPTER 32
(1959)

At the hospital, Theresa was placed in a wheelchair and wheeled into a room. A woman asked a series of questions about her medical history, and another nurse helped Theresa into a gown. Pains came about fifteen minutes apart so, Alice presented a deck of cards to fill the time.

After several hours, Theresa became more uncomfortable. "I don't feel like playing anymore. Sorry."

"You're just tired of losing," joked Alice.

Periodically, staff monitored Theresa's progress. "It won't be long now," they told her more than once.

The next day, she spoke to her morning nurse. "If I could just stand and walk—"

"The doctor wants you to stay in bed."

"But, I know—"

The nurse shook her head.

Theresa followed doctor's orders despite sensing a walk down the hallway would bring the baby sooner.

Alice came in looking refreshed. She had gone home for some sleep and a shower. "You're still here?"

Theresa breathed through another labor pain, her face damp with sweat and dark circles under her eyes. "I want this kid out of me."

"The lady at the desk said it won't be much longer," said Alice.

"They've been telling me that for two days."

Alice wiped Theresa's face with a cold rag. "You're okay."

"Yeah. You haven't had one of these, yet," Theresa snapped. Another contraction overcame her. "Oh...Can you get somebody?"

Alice hailed down a nurse who checked Theresa again. "I'll get the doctor." She left and returned with the physician.

He examined Theresa. "You're ready."

The nurse turned to Alice. "You'll need to step outside now."

"No problem there," said Alice. She patted Theresa's arm. "I'll let Jackie know. Good luck."

Her bed was prepared and moved to the delivery room where Theresa was instructed to curl up. Too tired to even argue about how to do that, she did her best to comply, and she received an injection in her lower back. After a few minutes, the saddle block took effect and the excruciating pain subsided.

A nurse assisted Theresa in positioning her body, and a large mirror was turned so she could watch. The intense sensation to push that huge thing out of her body overcame her and she began pushing. When the baby crowned, Theresa's glimpse of her first child was a tuft of brown hair. Mixing with the sweat drenching her face, came tears of amazement and of relief when the birth happened quickly. Then she heard the most unbelievably miraculous sound—a little cry.

The doctor placed the warm newborn on Theresa's chest. "You have a beautiful little girl."

As he cut and tied the umbilical cord, Theresa stroked the baby's face wondering how she would ever find the strength to release that little life. No, she was not for her. She was a gift. A gift for someone else. Tears filled her eyes.

Another nurse picked up the infant and whisked her away. "Let's clean you up, honey. Mommy's going into recovery."

Fatigue overwhelmed Theresa and she immediately fell asleep. When she woke, she lay in a ward with four other new mothers. One slept soundly as the other three chattered about their new babies.

A woman with green eyes said, "We're thinking about Kathryn Ann, but my husband's not sure."

Another woman with a splotchy face added, "We're naming mine after my grandfather, Gerald."

The mother with a yellow bandana around her hair shook her head. "I don't know. We can't seem to agree on anything."

"Well, you'd better hurry up," said green eyes. The women chuckled.

Splotchy face realized Theresa was awake and attempted to draw her into the conversation. "What are you naming your baby?"

Theresa turned her back from the other women and pressed the call button. This arrangement would not work. She couldn't be with those other women.

"I was in labor for only two hours. This is my third," said yellow bandana.

Green eyes rolled her eyes. "You were lucky. It took me seventeen."

Splotchy face lifted her hands. "Well, this was my first and—"

The women stopped talking when an older nurse entered the room and walked to Theresa.

Noticing her name tag, Theresa kept her voice low. "Betty, I want to be in a private room."

"But you're assigned to this room."

"You don't understand. I must have my own room."

The nurse scowled and shook her head. "That isn't possible."

The other women watched in silence.

Theresa's voice grew louder. "Look, you need to get me my own room, now."

Betty huffed then snapped back. "Raising your voice is not necessary. I'll speak with the doctor but I'm sure he'll say no."

Theresa faced away from the shocked mothers as they continued talking.

"Gee."

"What's wrong with her?"

"How rude."

Theresa pulled the pillow around her head until the women's comments were muffled and indistinguishable. How could they understand?

In a quiet room with a second empty bed, a kindly young nurse named Frances propped Theresa up. "There you go. I'm going to bring in your daughter so you can feed her."

Theresa waited in anticipation. This was what she had insisted on doing all along.

Frances came back with the bundled newborn, put her in Theresa's arms, and handed her a bottle. "I'll be back," she said.

Theresa caressed the tender, soft forehead looking at the baby's minute features. "So, you're the one that's been rolling around." She could not help but allow herself to revel in the closeness to the human who had lived inside her tummy for nine months—the one that had come from a few moments of drunken passion.

The baby fussed, and Theresa rubbed the rubber nipple gently on her lips enticing her to latch on, taking in the nourishment. In no time, the baby's eyes closed and she fell back to sleep.

Frances reentered and smiled. "They do get worn out. Do you have a name, yet?"

Theresa shook her head as the nurse took the infant back. "You should rest, too. I'll bring her back for her next feeding."

Unable to relax, Theresa could not ignore her longing that something would be wrong with the baby. Something that Theresa could believe to be unacceptable by adopting parents and making the child only lovable by her birth mother. Just one defect that would provide her a reason not to go through with the adoption. She sighed and mulled over what must happen the next time the baby was put in her arms. Only if she's perfect, would she give her up.

Frances returned for the second feeding and when she left the room, the infant took the bottle easily. Theresa removed the blanket, gown, booties, and two cloth diapers. The naked baby lay very contently across Theresa's lap. Then the task began.

She counted fingers and toes, stretched out the baby's arms and legs, massaged her scalp, and inspected her tiny ears. Theresa searched desperate to find something amiss, a single blemish, one imperfection. But, there was none.

She slipped her finger inside the newborn's curled fist, breathed in her fresh powder scent, and tried to speak. Only a cracked whisper came. "You are perfect." She struggled to process her conflicting emotions—grateful the baby was healthy, yet sad because there was no reason to keep her; no excuse. Another goodbye.

While putting the cloth diapers back on, she stopped. She needed to have something that touched her precious girl. Taking one of the diapers, she tucked it under her pillow.

Theresa redressed her in the single diaper, gown, booties, and rewrapped her in the blanket. She kissed her baby's creamy pink cheek and summoned the nurse, no longer trying to hold back her tears as she cradled and rocked her little one.

The young nurse rushed to the bed. "Theresa, what's wrong?"

Theresa shoved the baby towards her. "Take her."

Accepting the infant, Frances responded with concern. "Are you having problems feeding her?"

"Please, take her away."

"I could help you—"

"No. Just leave," Theresa yelled and the baby started to cry.

Frances frowned. "You've upset her."

Betty, the grouchy nurse from before, stormed in the room. "What's going on?"

The younger nurse seemed confused as to what to do. "She says to take her baby."

Theresa was almost hysterical. "Take her away from me."

"Do you want your child or not?" said Betty in a harsh tone.

Theresa covered her face and shook her head.

Betty pointed to the door and Frances carried the wailing baby out of the room. She came close to Theresa. "What a rotten mother you are! This is what happens to loose women like you. You don't care about who you sleep with, then you have these innocent children that you just give away to strangers. Shame on you."

Theresa shouted through her sobs. "You don't know anything about me."

"I know enough."

"Get out," screamed Theresa.

Betty removed a syringe from her pocket and walked to Theresa who pulled her arm away.

"Hold still," the nurse said sternly. Too upset to fight any longer, Theresa allowed the needle to slip into her arm. Betty stormed from the room.

Theresa's eyes sagged from emotional and physical exhaustion. She reached for the bedside phone and dialed. She managed to say the needed words. "Please, come take me home now." She barely hung up before falling into a sedated slumber.

A few hours later when she awoke, Jackie and Aunt Mable were seated in her room. Jackie got up and took hold of Theresa's hand. "Hey sweetie. How are you feeling?"

Theresa stared at nothing. The emptiness was suffocating.

A woman entered the room and set a paper and pen in front of Theresa. "We need permission for someone besides yourself to remove the baby from the hospital. And, you must give her a name for the birth certificate."

Theresa locked eyes with her best friend in the world and with no hesitation she responded to the nurse. "Her name is Jackie."

The next few days were spent at Jackie's house. Theresa's tears were plentiful and seemingly endless as she mourned her loss. She wondered how the adopting parents were doing with their baby. Her imagination painted pictures of joy and happiness of the new family—Catherine feeding and changing the infant, and Edward bragging at work about his new daughter.

Four days after Theresa had delivered, she knew she must follow through with her previous plan. She picked up a stack of papers she had written while at Phil's house, ones containing thoughts, feelings, and hopes for her daughter, and threw them all in the trash. Life must move forward for all of them. She contacted Chapman College, and when her daughter was seven days old, Theresa started student-teaching summer school.

Six months later, she traveled to the courthouse to finish off the adoption paperwork. Theresa stood staring at the documents for a long time. Her life had returned to normal and a wave of guilt and sadness rose up ready to consume her. There would no longer be any hope of seeing her little girl again. She stuffed it all down, deep inside, and penned her name to the papers.

CHAPTER 33
(2006)

Theresa used a tissue to blow her nose. "With that signature went all my rights to my firstborn daughter. Legally, she was no longer mine."

Darcy and Liz sat riveted. Their eyes as watery as Theresa's.

"I had grown to love her, but I gave her up to be loved by someone else. I made the decision with such agony, but also with courage that could only have come from God."

Liz wiped her eyes. "Did you regret it?"

"I only felt sorry for myself missing out on watching her become a woman. I thought about her many times…Can we take a quick break?"

Both girls nodded.

Theresa walked out to the warm sunshine and stood by the side of the building where she lit up. She closed her eyes as she inhaled and exhaled, the smoke billowing up around her. Even after forty-seven years, she couldn't share that part of her life without becoming emotional.

After she finished, she went back into the shop to where Darcy and Liz waited patiently. She sat down. "Sorry."

"No worries, Ms. Clavin," said Darcy. "Is that when you started smoking?"

Theresa nodded. "After the birth."

"Do you still have her diaper?" asked Liz.

"Of course. I keep it in my cedar chest. For the first several years on her birthday, I'd bring out the diaper and hold it close to my heart, remembering. Though you never forget these types of experiences, after a while you learn to deal with them and move on with your life."

Darcy typed more notes on her laptop. "What happened with Stephen?"

"I sent him a newborn picture. On the back, I wrote that this was his child whom he would never meet. Cruel, I know, now. But…" She shrugged.

Liz shook her head. "Who cares. He was a jerk to you. So you never saw the baby, again?"

"I did not. Phil remained faithful to his promise to watch out for her. He called me periodically to say everything was going fine. He didn't give many details, only a few things."

Darcy leaned forward. "Like what?"

"Things he thought would make me feel better."

"Can you tell us anything?" asked Liz.

CHAPTER 34
(1959)

Phil glanced up from the book he was reading to six-year-old Robby when the front door opened and in walked Catherine with Edward following. She cradled a pink blanketed bundle in her arms.

Robby sprang to his feet and ran to his mother. "Lemme see, lemme see."

"You have a baby sister," said Catherine as she sat down on the couch and Robby clamored next to her. "Remember what we talked about? We must be careful."

Her son nodded. "I gotta sister now, Uncle Phil."

Phil stood and walked over to shake his brother's hand. "Congratulations."

"You were a part of this," said Edward. "Thank you."

Catherine pushed the infant up towards Phil. "You want to hold her?"

He shook his head. "It's been a long while since I held one of those."

She put the baby in his arms. "You don't forget."

Within a moment, all Phil's fatherly experience returned. "What have you named her?"

"Yeah? Robbina?" said Robby and he started to belly laugh at his suggestion.

Catherine tickled his ribs. "No, silly. Melissa Nancy."

Phil nodded and stroked Melissa's tiny rosy cheek. "Hello, little Melissa. I feel like I already know you," he whispered. His eyes teared and he handed the baby back to his sister-in-law. In that moment, he was grateful for his nephew's distracting enthusiasm.

Robby bounced up and down. "Can I show Melissa her room?"

"Settle down," Edward told his son.

"But I want her to see all her new toys."

Catherine chuckled. "Alright, let's go."

(1964)

Phil knocked on the kitchen door, and Catherine answered.

She gave him a hug. "Hi. Come on in."

He set the white box he was carrying on the counter, and Catherine motioned for him to peek into the family room. He went and stood by the door.

Edward sat on the sofa with five-year-old Melissa wiggling on his lap. Her dark brown eyes matched the color of the long bouncing ringlets pinned back from her face with two red plastic barrettes.

"Tell me again, Daddy, pleeeze."

He laughed at her incessant giggling and pleading. "Okay, but this is the last time for today."

Melissa clapped and sat up straight.

Edward donned a solemn face. "One day Mommy and I were driving along the road when we suddenly saw something in the ditch. We picked it up, washed it off and found it was you…."

He stopped when Melissa put her hands on her hips and frowned at him. "No, no, no. Tell me the *other* real story."

Still in the doorway looking in, Phil stifled his laughter.

Edward winked at Melissa. "All right. Most Mommy's and Daddy's don't get to choose who their baby will be. But Mommy and I were very lucky because we got to pick you out of all the other babies."

Catherine quietly snuck up next to Phil, and together they eavesdropped. Melissa's eyes widened as she listened to the story her father had repeated many times over.

"We looked and looked at all the babies at the hospital, and they were all cute. The nurse said, 'Do you want this one?' And we said, 'No, we want that one,' and we pointed at you. Then she said, 'Do you want this one?' And we said, 'No, we want that one,' and we pointed at you."

Phil watched a grin slowly grow on his niece's face.

Edward continued. "She said, "How about this one? We said, 'No, we want that one,' and pointed at you. The nurse asked us about every single baby in the nursery, but we said we only wanted you. So we picked you from all the other babies."

Melissa giggled and fell backward on the cushions. "Tell me again, Daddy…pleeeze!"

"Nope, that was the last time," said Edward smiling and shaking his head.

Phil entered the room. "Who would ever want that kid?"

Melissa turned, squealed and ran full force at him. "Unca Phil."

He scooped her up in his arms and swung her high in the air. "Hi, sweetheart."

"D'jou bring donuts?"

"Just for you."

"Hey," came a protest from eleven-year-old Robby from behind.

Phil laughed and patted him on the back. "You too," he added. He put Melissa down and the kids bolted for the kitchen, the adults following.

Robby opened the box of goodies, and both he and his little sister selected their favorites—Robby a chocolate-filled maple bar, and Melissa a multi-colored donut.

Phil leaned down and carefully fingered the cross around Melissa's neck. "What a pretty necklace you have."

"Tank you," she said, her cheeks sticky and adorned with pink, red, and yellow sprinkles. "Mommy says it means God loves me."

Phil and Catherine exchanged warm smiles.

CHAPTER 35
(2006)

"Aw, how cute," said Darcy.

Liz leaned forward. "So cool about the necklace. I mean her adopted mom giving it to her."

Theresa nodded. "Eventually, Phil stopped calling. I think he began sensing it was difficult for me to hear about her."

Liz tilted her head. "That must have been hard."

"At first. But by then, I was married and had started a new family."

"Did you ever get to meet her?" asked Darcy.

Theresa checked her watch and exhaled. "I'm exhausted. Probably good enough for today. You girls still up for our final session?"

They both nodded together, packed up their things, and went on their way.

Theresa wanted to feel sorry for herself because she deserved it after all she went through, right? On the drive home, she smiled at her desire to feel bad, but everything had been so long ago. From her slouch, she straightened up and turned on the radio to catch up on the latest news report.

The next afternoon, after Theresa, Darcy, and Liz were settled with their typical hot drinks, and a massive frosted brownie with three forks. Theresa began.

"When Melissa was twenty-one, I really wanted her to understand what happened around her adoption, and that I didn't just abandon her. On my next visit with Jackie, we discussed it. I wasn't totally convinced I should interfere in Melissa's life."

"I'm sure she'd love to meet you," said Liz.

"Jackie thought so as well. She and Ben had been divorced for many years, but she called and talked to him. Edward still worked for the same company and Ben knew how to reach him. Within a few days, Ben reported back that Edward spoke to Melissa and she was very interested in meeting me."

Darcy gleamed. "Wow, that's amazing."

Liz put her hand over her mouth. "How scary."

Theresa agreed with Liz. "I decided to start by writing her a letter."

CHAPTER 36
(1980)

Theresa spent a whole evening with paper and pen in hand. She started and stopped several times, struggling with how to begin the first letter to her firstborn child. What should she even say?

> December 29, 1980
>
> My Dearest Melodie.

Maybe that was too endearing. She wadded up the paper and started again.

> Dear Melodie.
>
> I was told many years ago that was your name, but I'm still not too sure. I called you 'Jackie' when you were born and in my mind for the last twenty-one years.
>
> A letter of this kind is exceedingly hard to write. Words don't seem to fall into place easily. My mind is a mud-puddle of what questions you may want answered and still I'm not quite sure of what you really want. I hope that we can get together, if this is your wish, and talk sometime in

the near future. But, until then, I must proceed with what is uppermost in my thoughts and heart concerning your birth.

I have known and talked with many adopted children in my teaching career and their uppermost concern seems to be that of "not being wanted" and therefore "being given away." Realistically, this does happen sometimes. In our situation, this couldn't have been farther from the truth. Thus begins our story.

Theresa wondered if there were certain things she should not include, like how she almost used abortion as a way to escape her pregnancy. No. She should know it all. Theresa told her daughter about her unsuccessful trip to Los Angeles, and how being labeled as a 'bad girl' combined with immense feelings of hopelessness, had almost pushed her to suicide. She described her time with Phil.

I'm sorry you could not have known Phil in your adult life. He was a warm, understanding, kind man, and he loved you long before you were born. He loved and cared for me as a father would have his own child. I thank God he was there. I asked if he'd give you a small gold cross. I don't know if you have it or what happened to it, but it meant that both God and I loved you.

A tear dropped onto the paper and Theresa blotted it away. She described her experiences in the hospital during the birth and afterward in the privacy of her room.; how she kept the diaper and let her baby go.

Giving you up was truly the hardest thing I have ever done in my life. All this will not answer a lot of your questions, I'm sure. It may only raise more. It is a starting place. If you wish to know more or know me and my family as we are now, I don't know. I will tell you that you have a half-brother, seventeen, and a half sister, sixteen, that are aware you are out there somewhere. I am now an ancient forty-four years.

Theresa stopped writing. She chewed on the end of her pen reflecting on how naive she had been to have believed that a child needed two parents in order to be loved and raised properly. She shook her head and leaned back in her chair. That lesson had come at great loss. Eventually, she would share the story about her first husband dying at the age of thirty-two and how Theresa ended up raising their two young children by herself.

She turned to the fifth clean sheet of paper thinking this might be too much for a first letter.

I will stop this lengthy story amid old tears with this thought for you. Your parents, for that is what they truly are, have my deepest appreciation for your loving upbringing. They have given to you what too many children never have had—a home, guidance, and steady loving hands. A mother or father is not made by the fact of birth alone. A mother and father are 'grown' over the years of raising and caring for a child. I did not interfere and I will not interfere with your love of them or theirs for you. I do know, however, that there is room in all of us for adding another love. Please accept mine, as it has always been there even though you were not aware of it.

You are free to write me or call if you would like. I would like to know you.

With Love, your other mother, Theresa

Come almost midnight, Theresa read the latest version of her six-page handwritten letter. She sighed. The words would never be perfect or good enough. How could they be?

She would not re-write again because the letter must go in the mail, so she wrote on the envelope the address Ben had given her. Several weeks had already passed since her daughter said she would like to meet her. She may be wondering if her mother was ever going to get in contact.

In the morning on the way to work, with a flutter in her heart, Theresa dropped the sealed envelope in the mail.

Two weeks later, after a long day working at the local newspaper, Theresa opened her mailbox and amongst the advertisements and bills, there was a return letter from her daughter.

CHAPTER 37
(1981)

Theresa brushed her fingers over the return address and the name Melissa Gerhart. She did not know her first name, as Phil kept those details to himself when sharing his few stories long ago.

Her heart beat faster as she walked into her house. She didn't open the envelope right away wanting to revel in the anticipation. Admittedly, she held some apprehension on discovering who her baby girl had grown up to be. With no influence on this twenty-one-year-old woman, all the normal parental worries arose. Theresa hoped that Melissa had not become mixed up with drugs, hung out with the wrong crowd, or fell madly in love with some man who didn't truly care about her.

She tucked the envelope behind a framed family photograph on her dresser and changed clothes. Theresa fixed dinner for her son and daughter, and spent the evening going through her regular routine, although fighting an upset stomach. Once her children settled in their rooms for the night, she put on her nightgown, took the letter, and crawled into bed to read it.

After unsealing the envelope, a photograph tumbled out to the bed covers, picture side down. She left it turned over wanting to read her daughter's words first.

January 15, 1981

Dear Theresa, it's kind of strange to start this way, but I don't really know what I'm supposed to call you. I understand your difficulty now in writing a letter like this, I'm feeling the same way. I guess I should tell you right away, and hope to reassure you, that I never thought I was unwanted.

Theresa squeezed her eyes shut to keep the tears from coming out. She didn't want to start crying yet, it made it too hard to read the words.
"You weren't unwanted," she whispered.

My parents never kept the fact from me that I was adopted, and I appreciate that. It seems like I've always known and have been very open about it. When my friends and I get on the subject, I explain to them that I have the greatest respect for Theresa (as I was told your name was), and that the strength and courage you showed by giving me up, proved you were an exceptional person, and one with an extremely unselfish love.

Unsure if she agreed with that statement, but thrilled to read it, she turned to the second page.

But, even though my home life has always been happy, my feeling for my 'unknown' natural mother was one of great curiosity. The biggest part, I guess, was and still is (for a while longer), what you look like. I was told by a very dear old man, that I looked like you, if I looked into a mirror I would see your face.
That dear old man is my Uncle Phil. Theresa, he has not died. He's alive and living in Oregon.

Theresa gasped. Phil was alive?

> He never forgets my birthday or any other occasion. And, he speaks very highly of you. You were very special to him. He is by far my favorite uncle. He always has been and now I understand why I was his favorite niece. I was a part of you.
> Last February when I saw him, we got on the subject of you. I hadn't known much before, but he revealed a lot for me. I asked if he knew how to get in touch with you. Unfortunately, all he knew was that you were up north somewhere.
> I talked with a few of my close friends and we tried to figure out ways to find you but we didn't know your married name. Then months later, right out of the blue, my father received a call from Ben (I believe that was his name). I knew right then and there, that my curiosity would soon end.
> I believe my parents brought me up very well and that I'm pretty emotionally stable and open minded. I feel I've been very fortunate not only that you wanted to contact me, but because you have thought of me through the years. I have no doubt that we could become great friends and share a very special love.

Theresa touched the words written by Melissa, 'very special love.' Could this be real? Actually happening?

> When I got your letter, I sat and looked at it for a long time. As I read it...I cried. Not an unhappy cry, mind you, but an overjoyed sob. I had answered a great question in my mind. I had found my natural mother.

Oh, by the way. Melodie was close to my name Melissa. But, I would like you to know that if you want to call me 'Jackie,' it wouldn't bother me a bit.

I guess I will close now, but not in lack of things to say. I've so much to tell you about my last twenty-one years, and I've so much to ask you of yours. I've included a recent photo.

My mom had the gold cross and gave it back to me. It seems more beautiful to me now than ever before.

Take care, and I hope this is just a beginning of what is to come.

Love, Melissa (alias Jackie)

Her face dripping with tears, she gasped when she looked at the photo. "My daughter's beautiful." Gently she stroked Melissa's face, just as she had done in the hospital the first time she cradled her.

Theresa got up out of bed and stood in front of the bathroom mirror comparing their two faces. There were definite similarities. The dark eyes, heavy eyebrows, and thick hair reminded Theresa of her own appearance back in her school days. Her heart felt warm recognizing in her daughter's bright smile and shining eyes, a young and innocent zest for life. That same zest Theresa experienced during her first year at Chapman College.

The other thing Theresa noticed was Melissa's skin color—a rich olive tone. That did not come from her mother. She put her palm to her forehead as she stared at her daughter's image. Italian descent. Oh dear Lord, definitely Italian...or more accurately Sicilian.

Could it be Theresa had been wrong about the father? She crawled back into bed and hugged her knees up to her chest. It was all so much to process. Best to just deal with one thing at a time. Besides, no one knew what happened with Tony over two decades before. She picked up Melissa's letter again focusing on the fact that, she held in her hand, a letter from her first-born daughter. She dialed the phone to call Jackie. After apologizing for calling so late, she read Melissa's letter to her best friend, and they cried together.

CHAPTER 38
(1981)

Theresa resided in northern California while Melissa lived in the southern part of the state. A couple months went by during which they exchanged a handful of letters.

At last, Jackie convinced her friend to travel down to meet Melissa in person. "You can come to my house and bring your kids. She deserves to know her 'other' family."

Theresa alternated from sitting to pacing back to sitting in the front room of Jackie's home waiting for Melissa to arrive.

"Mellow out, Mother," said Jeff. "You're making me dizzy."

Mary put her arm around her mother's shoulder. "Shut up, Jeff. She's gonna love you, Mom. Don't worry."

Theresa's stomach churned as she longed for that love, but it still remained uncertain. Gnawing on her lip, she stood. "I need a cigarette."

Her daughter smiled. "Oh Mom."

The doorbell rang and Theresa froze. Time was up.

Mary and Jeff both peeked out of the window trying to get a first glimpse of their half-sister as Jackie walked to the door and opened it.

Theresa couldn't see anything but heard the short exchange.

"You must be Melissa."

"Are you my mother?"

Theresa chuckled to herself. She had sent Melissa her photograph, but the simple mistake of identity made Theresa realize that her daughter was just as nervous as she was for that initial introduction. How could she not be?

Jackie brought the young woman into the house. "Oh no, my name is Jackie, a longtime friend of your mother. Come on in and you can meet your family."

As soon as Theresa saw Melissa, the entire plan of what she would say left her mind. This was the child she had birthed. Now she was almost certain of the father. Theresa's memories of Tony and the act of Melissa's conception overwhelmed her. All she could do was return Melissa's stare.

The seconds grew awkward, and at last, Theresa snapped out of her silence. She stepped forward and embraced Melissa tightly. "My dear, so good to finally meet you."

"Yes. You, too."

Theresa released her grip and wiped away an escaped tear. With trembling hands, she motioned to her children who stood on either side of her. "This is your brother, Jeff. He's seventeen."

Jeff gave a little wave. "Hello."

Mary rushed over and gave Melissa a warm hug. "I'm Mary. You're my big sister."

Theresa loved her youngest daughter's elation. "Mary's sixteen."

"Hi," said Melissa.

"I recall seeing you right after you were born," said Jackie.

Theresa stared at her friend. "You did? I never knew that."

Jackie shrugged. "When we came to pick you up, I snuck a peek in the nursery." She winked at Melissa. "You were a cute little thing."

Melissa smiled, but the conversation died. Theresa felt the moments getting heavy.

Jackie broke the tension. "Why don't we sit."

Everyone took a seat—Theresa next to Melissa on the couch.

"I hope your parents aren't angry with you for coming," said Theresa. "I would never want to interfere."

"My parents were kind of worried at first. My brother, Robby, was adopted too. I guess he had a bad thing happen."

"I'm sorry to hear that," said Theresa.

"Yeah. When he was eighteen, his biological mother walked right into our garage saying she wanted to see her son. I don't know all that happened, but it didn't turn out very well. But, I made sure my parents understood that wanting to meet you had nothing to do with them because they'd always be my mom and dad. And I showed them your letter."

Theresa nodded, wondering what they may have thought of all her past decisions. It didn't matter.

Melissa glanced around the room. "I was curious if I actually looked like anyone."

Theresa looked into the dark facial features of all three of her children. "And, you do." Everyone nodded in agreement. "Melissa, you've told me a little in your letters, but tell us more about yourself. What sort of things do you like to do?"

"Well, I'm in college full time and work at a bank twenty-four hours a week. I love to listen to music and me and my friends do a lot of camping and snow skiing."

While Theresa watched her daughter's animated facial expressions and exaggerated hand gestures, she remembered how Tony had always been full of physical energy as well.

After a long pleasant visit, everyone said goodbye with promises they would get together again.

Late that night, after the excitement of that first afternoon together subsided, Theresa lay in the same small bed she had slept in years before at Jackie's house—the one from when she was pregnant and then when she wasn't. She wept tears for herself at the loss of watching her daughter grow up, and at the missed opportunity of holding and loving Melissa physically. Yet, she was relieved and proud of the way Edward and Catherine had raised her to be such a grounded, lovely young woman—one responsible, respectful, and excited about life. She remembered how difficult it was to give Melissa up so many years ago. Now, she couldn't help but believe it had been the right decision.

A sickening guilt replaced her tears as Theresa thought about Tony. For so many years she had buried those feelings about what happened. No one knew except her—and Tony, of course. Perhaps she was wrong. Stephen could very well still be Melissa's father. Theresa had no actual proof. Sometimes kids ended up looking like aunts or grandparents or not like anyone in the bloodline at all.

Upon closing her exhausted eyes for the night, Theresa decided Tony's story was one she did not need to tell, at least not now. What good would it do to share that little detail, anyway? That tiny little detail.

CHAPTER 39
(2006)

Liz licked the last smudge of chocolate frosting from her fork. "So, did you talk all the time?"

"Not all the time, but some," Theresa said. "We'd write letters and call periodically to learn more about each other. It's actually pretty amusing some of the things we have in common."

"Like what?" said Liz.

"We both love candy corn and suffer from weak ankles."

The girls laughed. "Hang on," said Darcy. "The more interesting question is did you ever tell Melissa about her dad?"

Theresa sighed. "We all want to look good in our children's eyes—at least for as long as we can. I shared stories of Stephen with her and did not disclose anything about Tony, yet I did eventually share the experience with Jackie. She was all over me to talk to Melissa. But, I had no proof, and Melissa wasn't asking for anything more."

Darcy opened her eyes wide. "So, she still doesn't know?"

"You wanting to hear more?"

The students nodded in unison.

Liz raised her hand. "Definitely. You can't stop now."

Theresa enjoyed that the girls were so interested in learning the end of the story. "When Melissa was thirty-seven, she began mentioning Stephen in her letters. I managed to side-step the question for a few months, unsure what I would say about what I suspected. But she upset the apple cart when she called and asked me point blank."

CHAPTER 40
(1996)

Theresa dried her hands on the kitchen dish towel and answered the phone. "Hello?"

"Hi, Theresa."

Theresa sat down, put her feet up on the footstool, and settled in to spend some time with her first-born child. She loved that their relationship had developed into a nice, warm, special one. "Hey daughter, how are you?"

A ten-minute catching up on life conversation ensued. Then Melissa said, "I want to ask you something."

"Sure."

"Um, yeah." Melissa fumbled with her words. "In my last few letters, I asked for more information about my biological father, Stephen, and you didn't respond."

Theresa's stomach dropped like a rock and she planted her feet squarely back on the floor. She had purposely chosen to avoid this particular subject.

"I wrote down his name when you first told me the story like fifteen years ago. I tried to track him down and found a phone number."

Theresa's hand flew to her forehead. No, no! She jumped up and paced across the room.

"I wondered if he'd want to meet me."

"You should not contact him," Theresa said, perhaps too quickly.

Melissa hesitated. "Well…"

"Please, tell me you didn't."

"I tried. But, the number was disconnected."

Theresa moved the receiver away from her face momentarily to let out a sigh. She plopped back on her couch.

"Do you have any idea where he might be?" asked Melissa.

Theresa wanted to wretch. No longer could she put it off. Now was the time to tell Melissa the truth, all of it. "I haven't been totally honest with you." Her heart pounded. "Stephen is not your father."

Melissa registered the claim through a gasp, a pause, and a, "What? How do you know?"

Theresa squeezed her eyes closed and imagined the photograph of Melissa in her initial letter and meeting her at Jackie's house years earlier. "The first time I saw you all grown up, I knew otherwise."

"But you told me all about Stephen."

She exhaled and hoped Melissa could or would understand. "I left a few things out."

"Obviously," said Melissa.

Theresa sensed well-deserved sarcasm. Why hadn't she told her sooner?

"So, who is my father then? Do you even know?"

A hollowness of guilt slammed into her gut. She readied herself for disappointment from her child. "Yes. His name is Tony."

"Why did you wait so long to tell me?"

Theresa swallowed. Where should she start? How about with the simple fact she just kept putting it off? Her skill at procrastination was not to be reckoned with. No, it had been deeper. The fear of rejection, ridicule, and judgment had kept that secret safely tucked away. Those same fears prompting decisions made in her youth had tagged along far into adulthood. "I'm not sure."

"Well, wow. I don't know what to say."

"I'm sorry."

The silence on the other end of the phone seemed unbearable to Theresa. Finally, she heard Melissa sigh loudly. "Okay. So, what does Tony look like?"

"Well, he's Italian—"

"Really?"

"Oh yes," said Theresa.

"I knew it," Melissa burst out. "All these years I told people I must have Italian in me. I mean, I'm short, talk with my hands, have an abundance of hair everywhere, and love pasta."

Theresa liked the change in Melissa's tone and chuckled at her stereotypical description.

"It was hard to believe that I came from a tall, blond-haired, blue-eyed Nordic man."

"I agree."

"So what happened with this Tony guy?"

Theresa tucked her legs beneath her. She explained about the invitation to sew curtains, the hesitant entry to the apartment, and how things rapidly progressed. "We both drank too much wine. I thought about leaving when things were getting out of hand, but I didn't. When I found out I was pregnant, I so wanted you to belong to Stephen, that I convinced myself that you did. The timing was right. Sixteen years ago, my error became clear. You belonged to Tony."

"Do you have any information on him?" asked Melissa.

Theresa rose. She walked to a small address book and opened to a dog-eared page. "I believe he's still in the same area, but I'm not sure what will happen when I tell him."

"Wait. You mean he doesn't know about me?"

She picked up her cigarettes and lighter, fiddling with them. "Not yet." Nothing came from the other end of the line. "I'll call him. I promise."

"Is Stephen aware that I'm not his kid?"

Theresa dangled a cigarette between her lips, badly needing to set it ablaze, yet she promised her children she wouldn't smoke in the house. "No."

"Why didn't you tell him?"

A tinge of well-aged revenge seeped into Theresa's voice. "I suppose it was my way of getting even."

"All these years this poor guy's been haunted by the thought that he has a daughter somewhere out there, but he's not my real father?"

Informing Stephen was an unresolved issue Theresa found no desire to resolve. "Don't feel too sorry for him, Melissa. If he held any interest, he could have found me through the college Alumni group, and he hasn't. Remember, his answer was abortion."

"True," agreed Melissa.

"It was easy for men to ignore things such as an unwanted pregnancy back in those days. With no DNA tests, girls dealt with their problems alone unless the father wanted to admit the situation and help with it."

Melissa blew out an extended audible breath. "Always full of surprises, aren't we?"

Theresa rolled the cigarette between her lips.

"Thanks for telling me," said Melissa. "I'm not mad, just really surprised. And glad Stephen didn't answer the phone."

She closed her eyes, thankful that once again, her daughter forgave her mother's actions. "I'll send you a few of Tony's school pictures from our yearbook."

"That'd be fun."

Theresa pushed to end the uncomfortable discussion early so she could finally inhale some calm and think. Once finished, she rushed to her porch and lit up. She had borne the entire guilt of that encounter for all those years, but it wasn't just hers anymore, it never was. Half of it belonged to Tony. He deserved to take his portion of it. Now he would. She would call him tomorrow, not tonight. She mulled over how to tell this man that he had a middle-aged daughter.

"God help me," Theresa muttered.

CHAPTER 41
(1996)

Theresa's eyes were glued to her telephone. She returned to her patio for another smoke, then came back inside. Uncertain how staring at the phone all afternoon could make this task any less torturous, she eventually picked up the receiver and dialed. It rang several times. Maybe she got the wrong number from her friend. Should she leave a message to call back or try again later?

"Hello," said a man's voice.

Theresa coughed, her throat dry. "Tony Arnetti, please?"

"This is he."

Tongue-tied, she internally screamed at herself to say something. "Tony, this is Theresa Clavin from Chapman College."

"Goodness, it's been a long time. How have you been?"

So friendly. He genuinely acted happy to hear from her. Too bad it wouldn't last long. She played along. "I'm good. How are you?"

"I'm doing pretty well. Life is busy, of course," said Tony.

"Indeed. Time goes by so quickly." Theresa paced in her kitchen, back and forth, as far as the phone cord would stretch, wanting to ditch the cliché small talk. "Hey, Tony, I'm calling because—"

"Are you helping to plan a reunion? That'd be a blast."

"No." She stopped walking. "I don't know how else to say this but to just say it."

"Alright."

"I'm not sure if you remember the wine we shared one time at college, but, well, you have a thirty-seven-year-old daughter." There, she said it. She counted as eleven seconds passed by while the news sunk in and he mustered up a response. God only knew how hard it must be.

"I think you made a mistake."

Theresa threw her arm up in the air. Not again. Why is it so hard for men to admit that consequences come from having sex? "Tony, she's yours."

"Are you sure?"

"Very sure."

"I can't talk now. Can you call me at work tomorrow?" Tony offered the phone number and hung up saying nothing further.

Theresa put down the phone receiver knowing he'd need time to process everything. When she went to bed that night, she remained awake only long enough to feel the burden lifted now that Tony knew the truth. She should have done this years ago. Now, sharing the details was all that remained. She slept like a log.

While standing in her kitchen the next day, Theresa called his work.

He answered pleasantly. "Good morning, this is Tony."

"Tony, it's Theresa."

The pleasantness disappeared. "Why did you call me at home? My wife was sitting right there."

"I thought that would be the best place."

"Please, don't call there again."

Theresa sat down, a bit confused. "I'm sorry, but I felt like you should know. I actually gave her up for adoption as a baby. When she was twenty-one, I met her in person."

"And you think she's mine?"

"No doubt about it."

Tony still sounded irritated. "If it's true, I don't understand why you didn't tell me sooner."

Theresa hesitated. "So much happened. When I saw her all grown up, I was certain you were her father. Her name is Melissa, and she wants to meet you." She heard dead air, so added. "Why don't I send you some information about her. You can let me know."

"Is she looking for something?"

Theresa laughed. "Oh, heavens no. I've known her for many years now, and she hasn't asked for money or anything. She's just curious."

After a pause, Tony said, "Go ahead and mail me the information but to my work."

She wrote down the address, and again, he disconnected without saying goodbye. Unsure how well he would handle everything, she wondered what she could send that would convince him knowing Melissa would be worthwhile. Melissa had been so excited at the prospect of meeting him. Theresa did not want her daughter to be disappointed by a rejection.

After a trip to the local print shop for some copies, she addressed a large manila envelope and started her letter, opening with another apology.

8/31/96

Dear Tony,

> I'm so sorry for the bombshell. But even unsuspecting parents have a right to know—and so do their children. If we had never drank that bottle of your Grandpa's wine, we'd still wonder what happened to those old college buddies. Yet, because of my inability to ever 'hold my liquor,' we created a common bond.

Theresa easily described the first meeting with her adult daughter, and how she realized Stephen was not Melissa's father. She chewed on the end of her pen. Harder were words admitting why she had not revealed his fatherhood years before.

> I suppose I did not tell you until now because I feared disrupting your life, and the possibility that you might reject her. Also, the chance you wouldn't remember me or the one time. She thought all those years that her father was aware of her when, in reality, you didn't have a clue she even existed. But, after so much time, who would hold anything against either of us?
>
> I'm enclosing a few things to provide you a clearer picture of what kind of woman she has become. She earned her master's degree. A smart one, huh?

She placed all the prepared items in the envelope: a newspaper article mentioning Melissa's activities during high school, an autobiography of her first twenty years of life written for a university assignment, a copy of Theresa's first correspondence with Melissa, and a recent photograph of Melissa with her five and eleven-year-old sons.

> Where I ever found the strength to give her up in the first place is beyond me. But it seems to have been the right choice for her, and I cherish the times we get to talk now and her acceptance of what is. After waiting for years on my

decision concerning her father, and then learning the fact I had lied—she still took me at my word that I thought it best for her. And perhaps best for you too at that time. Now, I hope it can be different and you two will be able to meet for I firmly believe that is truly all she desires.

Theresa stopped writing and went for a cigarette to gather her final thoughts. How could she say something useful while not scaring him off? Soon, the idea came and she went back inside.

If I can be of help in any way, feel free to call. There is no threat of my being involved in your life or causing you any difficulties. This is your decision, and although Melissa would like to meet you, it remains your choice. However, it could be an interesting life-learning experience for your children as it has been for mine. Mine now realize Momma is not always perfect.

As Ever, Theresa

She put down her pen and folded her hands. The last time she mailed a letter like this, the one to Melissa, she had received an extremely positive response. Theresa closed her eyes, hoping the same would happen once again.

CHAPTER 42
(1996)

Nine days later, Theresa and her daughter, Mary, busied themselves in the kitchen preparing to make strawberry jam from the fruit grown in their gardens. Theresa stood at the sink washing the berries as Mary gathered up the pots, jars, and other tools.

Theresa's telephone rang and since Mary's hands were dry, she answered. "Hello?... Hold on." A moment later, she held the phone out towards her mother and whispered, "I think it's him."

Theresa had been hoping for Tony to call and ask for Melissa's contact information. Her daughter was anxious to meet him. After a deep breath to calm her nerves, she accepted the receiver. "Hello?"

"Look, this whole ordeal has brought my marriage to the brink of disaster," Tony said, not sounding happy at all. "My wife is very concerned about our fifteen-year-old daughter and how it would impact her."

Theresa frowned in confusion. Why would that matter? "My daughter was around that age when she met Melissa. She did fine."

"I need to ask you a few questions," said Tony.

"Okay."

"Melissa was adopted, right?"

"Yes."

"Are her parents still alive?"

"Yes."

"Do they love her?"

"Yes." Theresa did not breathe as she waited for him to draw his conclusion. "Come on, Tony. Come on," she mouthed silently into the receiver.

"Then, she doesn't need to know me right now."

Theresa's chest burned and she closed her eyes. It was Tony's decision, but she never fathomed he would do this to their daughter.

"I'm sorry. Things are just too complicated," he said.

She opened her eyes and did not hide her curtness. "Well, she will be very disappointed. And, it will be your loss."

"I gotta go," he said and hung up.

Theresa gritted her teeth. And that's it? How could he simply dismiss his own flesh and blood? She turned to Mary. "He said, no."

Early the next morning, Theresa sat on her porch and smoked through the entire process of writing another letter to Melissa. She didn't want to perpetuate the anger she, herself, was experiencing, as that could only contribute to the pain of rejection she imagined her daughter would endure. She kept her words brief, hoping they would be enough.

Dearest Melissa,

Tony called last evening. He decided he cannot meet you. It's causing trouble with his wife. We should pull back as we can't force him to accept or deal with either of us.

There is really no point, nothing to be gained, only loss for him—at least from what he can see.

She could have written a book on how let down she was by Tony's decision. Her puzzlement on why he would so easily deny his daughter, no matter her age, and how Theresa now would carry more guilt not knowing if perhaps things may have worked out differently if she would have told him sooner. No, these were her struggles to wrestle with. How could she put a positive spin on things for Melissa?

> We stop here, knowing we tried to make our story have a happy ending. But, it already has one—we're both happy. So, you're stuck with me. We've dealt with the reality. Perhaps he will someday. I believe, even more firmly, that what I did in giving you up was right for us and right for your adopted family. I mourn missing your childhood, but I relish what we share together now. Reach out if you want to talk more.
>
> Love Ever, Theresa

Theresa sealed the envelope, figuring in a week she'd receive a call from Melissa and another opportunity to smooth things over. She had tried and failed with Tony, now she could do no more.

During the next five days, she fought a head cold. She slept a lot which helped her not think about Melissa's possible reaction to the news about her father. On the sixth day, she got the call.

After sharing everything through sniffles and sneezes, and anticipating either tears of denial or a barrage of rage, Theresa opened her mouth in surprise at Melissa's levelheaded, logical reaction.

"It is a letdown, but it sounds like the timing isn't right. Those three questions that he asked, makes me feel like maybe there will be a chance in the future that he might want to meet me."

Theresa hadn't thought about where Tony's questions had come from or why he had asked them. She smiled at how Melissa interpreted his response as necessary now, but also containing a sliver of hope. Her daughter had indeed inherited some of Theresa's own tenacity.

CHAPTER 43
(2006)

"I don't get why his wife didn't want him to meet his own daughter," said Liz.

"Yeah, she seems kinda mean," added Darcy.

Theresa shrugged her shoulders. "I didn't understand either, but I guess she had her reasons."

Liz leaned forward. "So did Melissa ever get to meet her dad?"

"Well, that's getting away from my story. That belongs to her."

The girls spent the next minute convincing Theresa to share. She really wanted to tell them what happened, but wasn't sure if their teacher, Stacy Hershey, would think it inappropriate.

Liz closed her laptop. "We promise not to put this in our paper, but we just have to know."

Darcy shut her computer as well and folded her arms across it.

Theresa laughed. "You two are pretty persuasive. Are you sure you aren't going into politics?"

They all laughed.

"Alright. My eldest daughter had picked up some of my stubbornness and determination. Three years ago, I received a call from Melissa. She had let seven years pass. This is our conversation and then how she described to me what happened with her biological father."

CHAPTER 44
(2003)

After several minutes of a general, catch-up type of phone call, Melissa made a bold statement. "I found out my work conference is in San Diego this year. So, I think seven years is enough time."

"For what?" asked Theresa.

"I'm going to meet Tony."

Theresa stopped peeling potatoes and leaned against the counter. "You are?"

"Yup. Time's up."

"Are you going to call him first?"

Melissa chuckled. "Nope. I'm just going to show up at his work."

Theresa rubbed her forehead. That could be risky—but admittedly interesting. "I don't know if that's such a good plan."

"Look, I can't tell him because it would be too easy for him to say he already said he didn't want to know me. I have to believe if I can meet him, he will see that I'm not a bad person."

A pierce stabbed through Theresa's chest. Is this what her daughter believed? "Oh honey, you're not a bad person."

"I know. But he at least has to acknowledge me."

Theresa nodded. "True. Are you going by yourself?"

"My friend Patti's going with me. But, I need to find out where he works."

At first, Theresa hesitated, but then complied, justifying the situation was out of her control. "The information's in storage. I'll find out and send it to you."

"Thank you."

Unable to avoid the parental advice, Theresa gave her warning. "You are an adult. I just don't want you hurt in any way, Melissa. I do understand your curiosity, and I'd want to do the same in your position, but I can't guarantee how he will react."

"I won't blame you if it doesn't work out," Melissa said. "But I've got to try one more time."

CHAPTER 45
(2003)

After searching the internet, Melissa sat in front of her computer holding a piece of paper with the name of a car dealership on it. She tapped her fingers to her mouth as she dialed the number listed and listened to it ring.

An operator gave a standard greeting.

Melissa had already planned what to say. "I wanted to come in next weekend and wondered if Tony Arnetti would be working?"

"It depends. He's off today, but I can put you through to his voicemail if you'd like."

"Um. Great. Thanks." She pushed the phone close and covered her other ear with her palm. She wanted to hear his voice, every intonation, every word. The line clicked a few times as her heart sped up.

A friendly man's voice played on the recording. "Hi, this is Tony. Please leave your name and number, and I'll call you when I return to the office. Thank you for calling."

When she heard the short tone, she quickly hung up. He sure sounded like a normal guy. She snickered at herself. What had she expected, an ogre?

A couple days before the visit to San Diego, Melissa called Tony's employer to check again. The operator confirmed that indeed, Tony Arnetti was scheduled to work on Saturday.

"Sweet," said Melissa to herself.

Melissa's brain buzzed with anticipation and excitement for the Saturday afternoon adventure. What would happen? How would he react? Would he remember what she looked like from the picture Theresa had sent him?

From the back seat of Patti's car, singing emerged from five-year-old, Amber. She stopped and asked. "Mommy, where are we going?"

"We're taking Auntie Melissa to meet someone," said Patti to her daughter.

Melissa was amused at Patti referring to her as Amber's aunt. Blood doesn't seem to matter when it comes to family.

Amber thought for a moment. "Oh. Who is it?"

"A person she hasn't seen for a while."

"Like ever," joked Melissa. "Thanks for going with me, Patti."

"No problem. I'm excited to see his reaction. Are you scared?"

"You could say that." Melissa shifted in her seat, fighting off the urge to request another stop at a gas station restroom. "Now remember, he's Italian. So if I end up missing in a few days, you'll know—"

"Oh stop," insisted her friend.

But honestly, Melissa didn't know much about this man. The thought of him being in the Mafia had entered her mind more than once since deciding to go.

Patti pulled into the dealership driveway and parked. They all got out of the car and walked to the main building.

Melissa took several deep breaths, making her slightly light-headed. "Oh man, I'm so nervous. I literally can hear my heart pounding."

They arrived at a small area with a palm tree hanging over green outdoor carpet. In the fake grass were three golf holes with a putter leaning against a bench. Amber instantly skipped around the little oasis.

Melissa thought the putting green was an ingenious way to keep restless kids occupied during negotiations for new cars or unexpected new father-daughter introductions. She was jerked back to reality when a young woman greeted them.

"Good afternoon. Can I help you?"

"Is Tony Arnetti, here?"

"Yes, he is. May I give him your name?

"Um. Patti," Melissa said not anticipating that question. The woman nodded and walked away.

Melissa scrunched up her face. "I'm a mess."

The lady came back almost immediately. "He's finishing up with a customer. He'll be out shortly."

Melissa sighed. More torturous waiting.

"Thank you," Patti responded for her dumbfounded friend, and the woman left. "Do you want to sit down?"

Melissa shook her head. Her mind raced. He'd see she was a good person. She knew it.

They both turned as an elderly salesman walked by them and through the door into the showroom.

"You think that's him?" asked Melissa.

"Naw. He's too old."

A thirty-something salesman exited the door and hurried by, giving them a polite smile.

"How about him?"

"Mmm. Too young."

An Asian salesman passed by while talking to customers. Melissa turned to Patti with a questioning face.

"I don't think so," Patti said.

Melissa was thankful for the humor. She chuckled, but only for a few seconds. A thin, middle-aged, graying man emerged from the building and headed towards them.

She rubbed her sweaty palms on her jeans commanding herself to keep breathing.

Melissa lowered her head, not sure what to do or what to say, her planned words making their escape. At almost forty-four, she was about to introduce herself to her biological father for the very first time. The one who seven years before had already said no to meeting her. This was her chance. Right now.

Tony approached and put out his hand, a broad smile causing the tips of his waxed, handlebar mustache to almost touch each other. "Patti, what can I do for you?"

She summoned the courage and looked at him straight in the eyes. "Actually, this is Patti." She motioned to her friend, then reached to shake his hand. "And, I'm Melissa Redmond."

Tony maintained eye contact. He also kept a hold of her hand. His mouth opened slightly.

Melissa felt sick to her stomach, her breath shallow. "Do you know who I am?"

"Yes, I know who you are."

"Are you mad that I came?"

"No. I figured you would come at some point."

Tony finally released her hand but kept gazing intently at her.

Melissa did not look away. Don't look away. She couldn't look away. Her toes curled inside her shoes. "I'm here for a work conference and thought I'd come by."

He blinked twice. "I'm almost done with a customer. Can you wait a few minutes?"

"Sure."

Tony turned stiffly and disappeared into the showroom. Melissa and Patti looked at each other.

"This is so surreal. He just held on to my hand."

"I can't imagine what he's feeling," said Patti. "I think he had tears in his eyes."

Melissa thought so as well. He was probably as nervous as she, plus he had no time to prepare for her arrival.

Amber engaged Patti in some kind of guessing game for the next several minutes. Melissa opted out. Tony hadn't sent her away. Not yet, at least. She kept watching the door.

After what felt like ages but no time at all, Tony reemerged. "Why don't we go into my office?"

Tony led Melissa, Patti, and Amber into a small room with a large glass window.

Melissa wiped her brow, certain she had sweat stains at her armpits. Why had she worn a stupid sweatshirt? She motioned to her friend. "Patti's my best friend from high school."

Tony shook Patti's hand. "Hello."

"Hi." Patti touched her daughter's head. "This is Amber."

Tony leaned down getting face to face and shook her hand. "Nice to meet you, Miss Amber."

Melissa liked his gentleness with the child.

"Nice to meet you, too," said Amber. "Auntie Melissa was really scared to see you."

"Amber," scolded Patti.

Melissa smiled, the five-year-old had been right on. A few moments of awkward silence filled the room.

"I think I'll take her outside," said Patti. "She's getting kinda squirmy."

"I am not," protested the perfectly behaved little girl. But her mother shuffled her out of the room anyway.

Tony sat down in his office chair with Melissa sitting across from him. He propped his elbows on the desk, folded his hands across his mouth, and stared at her. Again, she saw those watery eyes. She dug her thumbnails into the sides of her index fingers as she searched for something to say. "So, you've got a daughter?"

Tony appeared relieved by the question. He stood and unhooked a newspaper clipping attached to the side of a cabinet and handed it to her. "Sarah's twenty-one, almost twenty-two."

Melissa looked at the picture. Sarah stood partially bent over with a tennis racket gripped in her hands as if poised to receive a serve.

"She graduated from the University of Arizona. The college on your shirt."

Melissa glanced down at her sweatshirt. What a coincidence. She handed him back the article. "Obviously, she's a tennis player."

"An excellent one." He turned a framed photo of his daughter around so Melissa could view it.

What a proud father he was. A good sign. "She's very pretty."

"I also have two sons from my first marriage. One in the military and the other who lives about an hour from here."

"You got pictures?" She was curious to see if there were any physical similarities to herself or her own kids.

"Not here." After a short lull in the conversation, Tony began speaking quickly. "A few months ago I decided that I wanted to find out more about you."

Melissa raised her eyebrows and her shoulders dropped slightly. What? No way. He was interested in her?

"I returned everything Theresa had sent me, except for a paper you wrote in college. I couldn't remember Theresa's married name or which town she lived in, so I couldn't reach her."

From the back of his desk drawer, he pulled out a blue plastic folder with some items in it. As he continued talking, he removed the autobiography. "From your paper, I knew which university you attended, your high school, and your maiden name. I tried to get your married name from the university, but they wouldn't help. I found it by looking on your high school alumni website."

Hearing the excitement in his voice, Melissa's jaw dropped. She couldn't believe he had been searching for her.

Tony held up a printout of the home page from the credit union where she was employed. "From there I searched the internet to find where you worked, and then using the online yellow pages, I was able to track down where you lived." He lifted a printed map to her house, then raised his eyes.

She was unable to form any coherent words.

He straightened his posture and squinted. "I hope you don't think I'm weird."

Melissa broke into a smile. "No, no. I'm just so surprised you started looking for me right at the same time I came looking for you again, after all these years. I'm glad you actually wanted to meet me."

"I wanted to meet you seven years ago, but, well, the timing wasn't right."

She nodded. Her hunch had been right. It had all been timing.

His attention was drawn to a man who walked past his office door. He waved at him, and looked back at Melissa and grimaced. "I have a customer."

Even though she didn't want their talk to end, she picked up her purse. "I'm going to be in town at this conference all next week. Is there any way we can get together?"

Tony hesitated and his brows furrowed. "I can't tell my wife right now. It's just really complicated."

"I wouldn't want to do anything to create problems. If we can, fine. If not, that's okay." But it really wasn't okay. Not really. Wasn't he curious, too?

He took his card from a holder on his desk and handed it to her. "I'll see what I can arrange."

She made a note on her business card and gave it to him. "Here's the hotel where I'm staying."

They both stood.

Melissa ignored her trembling. "Hey, could we take a picture outside before I go?"

He answered right away. "Of course."

They went to the putting green where Patti and Amber waited. Melissa gave Patti her camera. "Can you—"

"Yes, yes."

Melissa stepped next to Tony. This was the first photograph with her blood father. It certainly wouldn't be her prettiest, but preserving the moment was more important. He unexpectedly put his arm around her, pulling her closer. Nerves had her toes curling like fists.

Patti snapped the photograph, then she and Amber said goodbye to Tony.

"Thanks so much," Melissa said to him, her mouth dry.

"Let me give you a hug." He wrapped his arms around her and she felt the dampness on his shirt. She wasn't the only one perspiring.

He moved back, keeping ahold of her shoulders. "We'll talk later then, okay?"

"Okay," she managed to say.

He gave her another squeeze before they parted ways.

Melissa chewed on her lip as she led Patti and Amber back to the car in silence. She knew things would change if she could just meet him. Brushing back her hair, she tried to appear unaffected by what had just happened. Maybe he was still watching her. Just chill, but how could she?

Once inside the vehicle, Patti burst out. "Well, what'd he say?"

Melissa's eyes were wide when she turned to face her friend. Her heart raced and body shook. "Unbelievable. He had a file on me with downloaded pictures, and he knows where I'm working and even where I live."

Patti scrunched her face. "Is that a tad bit creepy?"

"No. It meant he was looking for me right when I was looking for him."

"Amazing. So, is he a nice guy?"

Melissa nodded. "He honestly seemed happy I came."

Patti started the engine. "I want every last detail."

Melissa struggled to concentrate while listening to the conference speakers the following week. Her notes were cryptic and sparse as her mind wandered. She told every new acquaintance who would listen about finally meeting her biological father. Melissa and Tony swapped a few voicemail messages about lost sleep and difficulty in focusing on their daily tasks with so much to think about. The day before she was scheduled to leave, he left a message about picking her up from the hotel, spending an hour together, then dropping her off at the airport the next day.

Despite still feeling nervous, Melissa wanted to learn as much as she could about Tony since she wasn't sure if she'd get another chance. During their time together, Melissa asked about his family. He talked about his parent's immigration to the United

States from Sicily and drove her through the heart of Little Italy in San Diego where he had grown up.

Tony parked the car by the ocean and gazed out the window.

Melissa reached into her purse. "So any grandchildren?"

"Not yet."

She took a photo from her wallet and handed it to him. "Actually, you do have grandkids." She hoped he could experience some pride or a connection with her boys, even though he had never met them.

He looked at the photograph for a long time. "In the picture Theresa sent me, I saw your children and have thought a lot about them. They are handsome boys."

"My oldest son looks like you."

Tony returned the photograph. Melissa sensed he wanted to say more, and she didn't speak as she slipped the picture back into her wallet.

"After I found out all that information about you, I just sat on it, because I didn't know what else to do," Tony said. "So many times, I pictured myself sitting at my desk and you walking into my office. And, that's exactly what happened. I'll always cherish that moment when we first shook hands and I held your hand in mine."

She watched him blink watery eyes, making her do the same. Her throat constricted, and she swallowed away a lump.

"I really wish I could tell my wife, but I need to wait for the right time, and I'm not sure when that will be. She was very upset when I told her about you the first time."

"I understand," said Melissa. But, honestly she didn't. The encounter when she was conceived, happened between Theresa and Tony long before he probably even knew Linda. Melissa thought about her own close relationship with her father, Edward. One she would never jeopardize. He remained her father, as Catherine would always be her mother. Melissa just happened to have two sets of parents, now. But, doesn't everyone possess the capacity for more?

For a few moments, they both sat staring at the waves hitting the shore, then she turned to face him fighting off the rising fear of losing what she had just gained.

"I stuck with my belief that if I could meet you face-to-face, you would see for yourself that I wasn't spiteful or manipulative or after money," Melissa said. "Although, I'd love to meet your wife to show her I'm not a threat, based on her reaction before, I'm afraid she might act the same way, and I don't want that to happen."

Tony sighed. They locked eyes and hugged clumsily in the car. He glanced at his watch. "We've got to get you to the airport."

During the short drive, they didn't talk much.

Melissa stared out the front window trying to push the awful question from her mind. Would he say, that's it, it's too hard? Don't contact him anymore? What would she do? What could she do?

Tony pulled in front of the terminal and jumped out to retrieve Melissa's suitcase from the trunk. "I'm sorry we couldn't visit more," he said.

She refused to just leave without knowing if they had a future or not. "I was thinking, maybe we could email and call each other once in a while?" She held her breath. Would he reject her a second time? Or was meeting her once enough for him?

He looked thoughtful and nodded. "That's a great idea."

Melissa exhaled and smiled. He does want to know her.

After another hug, Tony kissed her on the cheek. "You're a good kid."

Warmth spread through her chest. Edward, told her that all the time. It was his way of saying he loved her. Pretty certain love was a bit premature with Tony, she chuckled. He's a dad.

He quickly got in his vehicle, waved goodbye, and drove away.

Melissa could not wipe away the smile on her face, and she looked forward to telling Theresa all about what happened.

CHAPTER 46
(2006)

"That is way cool," said Darcy.

Liz nodded her head.

"When she called to tell me how things went, I was ecstatic," said Theresa. "I was so glad the outcome turned out positive. Apparently, they corresponded through many emails and some phone calls for almost a year. That's also when Melissa started to call me Mom instead of Theresa."

Darcy frowned. "Why'd she wait so long? You are her mom."

Theresa had wondered the same, trying not to be hurt by the formality. "I supposed she just needed to get to that point on her own." She remembered the first time Melissa began her letter with, "**Dear Mom.**" It had been a good day.

"How'd her parents, I mean her adopting parents, feel about the whole Tony thing?" said Liz.

Darcy nodded. "Yeah. I mean you asked for permission to meet her. This was kind of different."

"Melissa told me that she waited for a while before telling Edward and Catherine that she had met Tony. She was afraid they might be upset, especially her dad. But they were alright with it. Her children were also very interested. Her youngest boy immediately asked if his new grandfather owned a Ferrari."

"Ha. That's funny," laughed Darcy. "Did he?"

Theresa shrugged. "Melissa said periodically she'd hint that it might be a good idea for Tony to tell his wife about their relationship, even though she was worried about what might happen. She had mentally prepared herself for his possible rejection when she first met him, but now they had established a bond, that would be hard to give up. But, he kept putting off revealing their secret."

"I'm sure everything worked out, though, right?" asked Liz.

"Not exactly."

Darcy leaned forward in her seat. "Did the wife find out?" Theresa cocked her head but did not speak. "Ah, come on Ms. Clavin. You can't not tell us now."

The girls sat, their eyes glued on her.

Theresa knew she couldn't leave them hanging. She waggled her index finger at them. "Not for the paper."

Liz crossed her chest and Darcy raised her palm.

Satisfied, Theresa nodded. "Melissa and her family were planning a California vacation to begin in San Diego. Her kids were excited to meet their new grandfather. A few days before they left, she emailed him about a dream she had. In the dream, Tony told his wife everything, and she showed up to meet Melissa as a happy surprise. Well, things in real life didn't quite work out so rosy."

CHAPTER 47
(2004)

Melissa received a page from Tony for her to call his work, but she knew he wasn't scheduled for that day. As soon as he answered the phone, she knew there was a problem.

"Things are extremely bad," he said.

"Why? What happened?"

"When you emailed me the other night about your dream, you know, the one where you and Linda met?"

"Yeah?"

He exhaled. "I took that as an omen and told Linda about you."

Melissa couldn't believe it. She'd been urging him to tell her for months knowing no way their secret could last forever. She did not expect him to come clean two days before her family trip to San Diego. "What'd she say?"

His voice caught. "Nothing's good, now."

Melissa sat down. This could be a problem. Not just for the upcoming visit but for any visit, ever. "She's bound to be mad because you haven't said anything for almost ten months."

"I told her you were my daughter and I wanted you and her to meet. But it backfired. She's so upset with me. She kept saying I didn't know for sure you were mine, and I should be concerned because your children are coming thinking they're being introduced to their grandfather, and what happens if I'm not?"

"You and I know you are."

"But, she doesn't. Linda's really angry with Theresa for doing things this way and having no proof."

"I am the proof." Melissa tried hard not to sound defensive. "I can talk to Linda if you think it would help."

"No," he said quickly. "Not a wise idea."

Melissa slumped back in her chair. Though she never saw a picture of tall, blond-haired, blue-eyed, Stephen, it appeared obvious to everyone seeing photographs of Tony and Melissa that they were related. She must protect what she and Tony had already established. "Let me ask you this. Is the bottom line of this whole thing that Linda needs proof?"

A moment of silence passed. "Yes. I think that's it."

"So, if it helps her accept things, let's do a DNA test."

Tony groaned. "I suppose we should. I'm sorry I can't see you. I was looking forward to meeting your family."

Despite her disappointment, she kept focused on him since he was the key to continuing their relationship. "Me, too. I mean, we all want to see you, but getting your marriage back on track is more important right now. Having positive DNA results will help."

"I hope so."

"Dad, I'm proud of you for telling her."

He sighed. "I'm the proud one. I've felt so emotionally strung out since this happened, and so worried about what to say to you. But, you didn't sway one bit, instead just asked how we could fix things. You're a problem solver, Melissa. I'm too much like the famous ostrich—burying my head in the sand to avoid dealing with anything. You tackled the problem in a matter of seconds. The same one I held inside for how many years?"

She smiled. "You may relate with the ostrich, but leave it to me to put my arms around your neck and yank you up for air. Thanks for staying with me."

"You're not the one who started this whole thing," he said. "I did that back in September of 1958. Which we will prove."

Her eyes filled with unexpected tears as she realized he didn't want to lose her either. "Please tell Linda I want to do the test so she can feel better about everything, and I appreciate her concern about my boys. I don't want to bust into your family or get anything. And I'd never want Sarah to think I'm trying to steal her dad away."

His voice shook. "I should go home."

She gave her best reassurance. "Please, don't worry. Things will be all right. After my vacation, we'll make arrangements for everything. I promise."

After Melissa and her family returned home, she coordinated the DNA tests. They both submitted cheek swabs to the laboratory. While they awaited the results, Tony called and she could tell by the tone of his voice that his home life was improving.

"Actually, things are lighter now everything's out in the open," he said.

She released a long breath. "Excellent."

"I'm calling to tell you about my entertaining afternoon."

Melissa closed her bedroom door to lessen the sounds from the video game in the next room. "What happened?"

Tony launched into his story. "My daughter, Sarah, had her vehicle at the dealership getting some repairs done. I was at lunch when she called and said she was there to pick up her car. I told her I'd put her keys in my office desk drawer. Apparently, when she went to find them, she also found a printed email from you with the instruction sheet for taking the DNA test."

Melissa grimaced. "Oh, no."

"Sarah left and called me again. She was livid. 'Dad, are you having an affair?'"

Melissa's hand clapped over her mouth.

"Of course, I denied it. 'Then who is Melissa Redmond?' I planned to tell her about you after we got our DNA results back and her mother was okay with everything. So I hesitated, which made me look more suspicious. 'Oh my God. You're cheating on Mom,' she said. I made up some lame explanation—something about Melissa being an old friend. But, Sarah's smart and she saw right through it. God, I looked so guilty."

He laughed which gave permission for Melissa to laugh out loud as well. "How'd you wiggle out of that one?"

"I finally decided to just tell her the truth. She was irritated and full of questions. 'What? I've got a sister? Were you ever going to tell me? Is there something wrong with her? Can I meet her? Do I look like her?'"

Melissa grinned.

"I told her there was nothing wrong with you. I simply wasn't aware of you for a very long time. She asked if her mother knew and I said she most definitely did. When I got home from work, I explained the whole story and how I only met you last year. She was still frustrated we never told her about you. She couldn't understand why it was such a big secret."

"Exactly," agreed Melissa. "Us kids don't seem to have the hang-ups like you parents do. Maybe your daughter can help her mother acknowledge the situation."

"You might be right about that. It will be a relief to get those test results so everything can be out."

Melissa exhaled. "I'm so glad I had the guts to find you. Taking the risk of being rejected a second time has been worth it. I don't even want to think about what I would have missed if you would have turned me down on the putting green."

CHAPTER 48
(2006)

Theresa brushed crumbs from the table onto the empty brownie plate. "One week before the anniversary of Melissa and Tony's first meeting in person, they found out they indeed were father and daughter. The DNA test was positive."

Darcy and Liz high-fived each other causing Theresa to smirk.

"So, Melissa took her family to meet the Arnetti clan, and she told me that Linda greeted her very warmly. Turns out Linda really wasn't angry with Melissa, but with me."

Darcy frowned. "Why mad at you?"

"Because I waited all those years to tell Tony, and then I just dropped it on him out of the blue."

Liz threw her hands up. "Well, she was the one—"

"No, she was right. I should at least have told Tony when I first met Melissa at twenty-one. But, what can I say?"

"Did you ever meet Melissa's adoptive parents?" Darcy asked.

Theresa shook her head. "Not yet."

"You should go," urged Darcy. "Aren't you curious?"

Curiosity or the need to bring everything full circle, Theresa didn't know which. "I wanted to take things at Melissa's pace and not rush or push her. I chose not to attend her wedding, even though she invited me. And, I didn't go for the birth of her babies as I felt her mother, Catherine, should have those privileges."

"Well, I bet they'd like to meet you," said Liz.

Theresa bowed her head. She hoped so.

A horn honked outside and Darcy looked at the time. "Oh. That's my mom. I'm sorry, Ms. Clavin. We've got to go."

The students unplugged and packed up their laptops as Theresa gathered and stacked the cups. "Thank you for listening to my crazy stories, girls. I hope you learned a few things about life. Especially that there is always room in a heart for one more loving relationship."

Liz slung her backpack over her shoulder. "Thanks for telling us, Ms. Clavin. It was totally amazing. We'll get an "A" for sure on this paper."

"No doubt," added Darcy.

Uncertain if the description of 'amazing' actually fit, Theresa decided not to dispute the claim. "Stay in school and be careful of the boys." She winked at Liz.

Liz nodded and the girls left with waves and goodbyes.

Theresa watched them exit with their belongings and climb into a large pickup truck. Her attention turned back to the now empty table. A pungent scent of grinding coffee hit her as it had at that same time the past few afternoons. She would miss sharing her tales and there were so many, many others. Maybe another paper, another time. The interview reminded her not only of her own journey but of all the other people involved along the way. When her cell phone buzzed, she fished it from her purse and answered. "Hello?"

"Hey Mom," came the familiar voice of her daughter. "You ready?"

"As ready as I'll ever be."

"Good. I'll see you, on Monday," said Melissa.

Theresa closed her eyes and took in a long, slow breath. The final step was near.

CHAPTER 49
(2006)

Theresa stood engulfed in cigarette smoke while inside a designated smoking room at the Phoenix airport. She exchanged small chit-chat with other nervous passengers.

"Here for fun?" a woman inquired as she lit up.

Theresa was uncertain how to answer. "My daughter lives here." She inhaled. "I'm meeting her parents for the first time." The woman's face contorted in confusion and Theresa added, "Her adoptive parents."

"Oh, I see."

A balding man with thick glasses stepped into the already crowded room of fellow smokers and stood in between the woman and Theresa, making any further conversation impossible.

Theresa didn't really want to talk to anyone, anyway. She glanced at her watch. Melissa would arrive in the next few minutes so she worked at finishing her second cigarette, trying to imagine for the hundredth time how the upcoming meeting of Catherine and Edward would go. What would they think of her? Had Phil told them anything about her? What had Melissa shared about the mother who had given up her child? Maybe they didn't really want to meet her.

She took the last drag and dropped the butt in a silver container, and looked at her watch again. Was there time for one more? Probably not.

Theresa tried not to admit to herself that, without her daughter's urging, she probably wouldn't have come. Melissa had wanted Theresa to visit Phil, but she had put that off for too long, and he died. Theresa didn't want Melissa to be disappointed in her for missing out on the opportunity to meet her parents.

She walked to the pickup area, her hair and clothes reeking of smoke. She'd definitely have to quit when she got home.

Theresa smiled and waved when she saw Melissa. She always loved seeing her daughter, even though the in-person visits were far less than she'd like.

Melissa pulled her car to the curb, got out, and embraced Theresa. "How was your flight?"

"Terrific, if you like being imprisoned in a room with windows you can't open."

After loading Theresa's suitcase in the trunk, Melissa turned to her. "Do you realize this will be the longest time we've spent with each other, ever? I hope you still like me after spending five solid days together."

"Well, my dear, we've spent at least nine months together and we got along fine, except for your constant hiccuping."

Theresa spent four enjoyable days with Melissa as she gained a glimpse into her daughter's life. They made a day trip to Sedona and sat on the balcony of a coffee shop looking out over the breathtaking red rocks.

"Thanks for finally coming to do this," said Melissa. "My parents are getting up there in years, and I really want you guys to meet."

"How old are they now?"

"My dad's eighty-six and my mom's eighty-four."

She knew Edward and Catherine were older than her. However, she had forgotten by how many years. Catherine could have been a young teenage mother to Theresa. She took a sip of hot chocolate. "I'm anxious about meeting them."

Melissa patted Theresa's back. "They'll love you." Isn't that what Mary had claimed when Theresa was to meet Melissa for the first time? She hoped it would be true.

Her daughter excused herself to use the restroom, leaving Theresa on her own. Here she was almost seventy years old and still missing her own Momma. She blinked rapidly dissipating the tears. And Harold went to his grave never knowing about Melissa, his first grandchild. Theresa never found the courage to tell him for fear of experiencing his judgment. Sad for him, sad for her.

Melissa returned and Theresa sat up straight.

"It's so gorgeous here," Theresa commented, although it was only a distraction. The dull ache in her stomach kept reminding her that the next day she must face Edward and Catherine.

Later that night, a knock came at the guest room door.

"Come in," called Theresa.

Melissa opened the door and entered. "Hi."

"Hi."

"I thought you might want to see this." Melissa held up the tiny gold cross necklace.

Theresa's chest tightened. "Oh, my." She touched the now dull cross remembering the day she purchased it and gave it to dear Phil, hoping it might communicate to her unborn baby what she herself would be unable to say.

"Thanks for giving me a chance at life," said Melissa. "After all you went through to get me into this world, and then all the wonderful people in my life, how could I think I wasn't meant to be here?"

Theresa swallowed and hugged her daughter. How could she ever have imagined this happening? Both hers and God's message of love had come through. "God certainly meant for you to be here."

CHAPTER 50
(2006)

Theresa made Melissa stop at a park a few miles away from Edward and Catherine's house, so she could smoke one more cigarette. "I need a minute."

She left Melissa in the car and walked to lean against a tree. Children played on the monkey bars and climbed the plastic structures, yelling and laughing. Soon she would meet the couple she had thought about for such a long time, especially when Melissa was young. She worried about what they would think of her. Would they ask her questions about her life? Might they make judgments about her decisions? Would they feel threatened by her involvement with their daughter?

Theresa sighed and returned to the vehicle. Time to get this finished. They drove to the Gerhart's home.

Melissa led her straight into the back entrance, no need to knock. A bell on the door jangled, announcing their arrival. Theresa wrung her hands together as they walked past a golf hat collection and a table full of photographs of Melissa and Robby's families. Regardless if they liked her or not, she was grateful they had been there back in 1959. That's what she'd tell them.

They rounded a corner, and Edward and Catherine stood there waiting. Theresa remembered seeing the photograph of them at Phil's house perhaps half a century before and she instantly recognized them. Edward a bit shorter from age. Catherine still petite and her hair heavier on the salt rather than the pepper. Both carried evidence of a long life on their faces. And, they were smiling at her.

"Mom, Dad, this is Theresa," said Melissa.

Theresa extended her arm and shook Edward's hand. She hoped he didn't notice her trembling. "Hello, Edward." She saw the glint of tears in Catherine's eyes as she took hold of her hands. "Catherine. I'm so happy to meet you."

"We are as well," said Catherine.

Theresa pushed down her tears, needing to get her words out before she couldn't. "I've waited forty-seven years to thank you in person for raising Melissa. You did a remarkable job."

"I want..." Catherine looked at Edward. "*We* want to thank you for going through with your pregnancy. Otherwise, she wouldn't have been a part of our family."

The women did not release their grip.

"Phil told me wonderful things about you both. He was such a kind man. While I carried Melissa, she really felt like a gift from God meant just for you."

"And a gift she was," said Catherine.

Everyone, including Edward, wiped an eye.

They spent the afternoon sharing family stories and perusing albums. Melissa's baby photo showed first, the one picture Theresa recognized. Then came pages of birthday parties, vacations, boyfriends, high school graduation, and other significant times. Theresa could only smile, nod, and blink back tears of joy and loss. Melissa had a full and complete life with a loving family—just as Theresa had prayed for her daughter.

As they readied to end their visit, Theresa excused herself to the restroom. From her purse, she slipped out a letter penned the night before. She wanted to read it one final time as it held important words, too difficult to convey verbally.

Dearest Catherine,

From the moment I decided to give my child to you, she became yours and not mine. I was only the vessel holding the prize that was to become the ultimate gift. How I wished during my pregnancy I could have shared with you the first flutterings of that tiny human being. I wrote to you of my feelings of love for the baby. I wrote of my concern that you give it a happy life—a life of caring and teaching it to care for others. Of my gratefulness for you in raising this child as your own, and she truly is your own. I wrote with reassurances I would never intervene in your lives. I'm sure there was fear those first months, and how I longed to tell you "it would be alright." I wrote many, many letters to you that were never mailed. After Melissa's birth, I destroyed them. Perhaps they should have been saved, but they remained a private part of me. I can only tell you all were filled with love for you and the child I carried for you.

Please accept my sincerest and deepest gratitude to you and Edward for raising your daughter so beautifully.

Theresa

Theresa swallowed. It would work. She put the note back in the envelope with 'Catherine' written on the front and propped it up against the ceramic soap dish. She checked herself in the mirror, hoping her red eyes would go unseen.

After all the goodbyes and hugs, Theresa and Melissa left. The ride back to Melissa's house stayed mostly silent in reflection. Happy she had gone, Theresa knew it had been her first and last talk with Edward and Catherine, and that was okay. A warm sense of closure bubbled in her body.

Later that afternoon at the airport, Melissa hugged Theresa tightly. "I love you, Mom."

Resting her head against Melissa's, Theresa squeezed her eyes shut willing herself not to cry, not yet. "I love you, too, daughter."

Melissa released her grip. "Let's talk next week."

Afraid to speak, lest the weakening dam broke and a flood emerged, Theresa waved and hurried through the sliding doors, suitcase in hand. Once in the airport terminal, Theresa immediately found a restroom and locked herself in a stall to weep. Was it a happy or sad cry? It didn't matter because she knew from years of experience, how those little droplets falling from her eyes released so much hurt and joy, trouble and gain. Although delighted with her relationship with her daughter, she accepted that she would never have the closeness that Melissa held with the parents who raised her. She had been Theresa's gift and you don't ask for a gift back. Yet, what a blessing to the heart when that gift is generously offered back to share with you. She'd been granted another chance to play a part in the life of her first-born child. What else could she have asked for?

Theresa arrived home and plunked down in her favorite chair on the patio. Her little patch of grass needed cutting and her garden was desperate for some attention. That could happen later. She lit a cigarette and stared at the tall, gray pines and cottonwood trees surrounding her house. Her body and mind were tired not only from the travel but from the emotional expenditure from all that happened over the last two weeks. The sharing of so many stories with young Darcy and Liz. The five-day trip to visit Melissa. Then, meeting Edward and Catherine.

Her sigh led to a cough. Perhaps it had been too much. Definitely, too much smoking. She tossed the butt in an old coffee can already overflowing with the evidence that she needed to get serious and give up the cigarettes.

She entered the kitchen and sifted through the stack of mail Mary had piled atop the counter. One eight-by-eleven inch envelope, addressed to 'Ms. Clavin,' intrigued her, so she ripped open the seal. Inside was a thank you note and a copy of the school paper written by Darcy Noble and Liz Valdez. The "A+" on the top of the page brought on a proud nod. She set the report aside, planning to read her story through the eyes of her young friends tomorrow, or maybe next week, or the week after.

Theresa brewed a cup of decaf and sat down with her feet propped on a worn footstool. It was quiet. She gazed around the room at her lifetime of mementos, and at her own pictures. Certainly a few of Melissa and her family but many more of Mary and Jeff, her other adult children. Also photographs of her grandchildren, great-grandchildren, and of Jackie through the years. She smiled at her multitude of experiences with friends and family and neighbors and students. Theresa found a way to make it through the worst and the best of times. Both heart-wrenching loss and unexplainable bliss.

She picked up a dusty frame with a rarely captured moment of herself and Ann, her mother. They stood in front of the cabin she had helped build over sixty years ago and during one of the few happy periods of her childhood. Theresa touched her mother's beautiful image. That image she never could forget. The one person who was never far away. "Momma," she said aloud. "I think I've grown up a bit more, today."

EPILOGUE
(2016)

Down to less than eighty pounds, Theresa felt that the size of the bed she lay in seemed excessive. Her roommate wasn't very pleasant, complaining to the staff and arguing with someone on the phone. Unable to speak herself, beyond an unintelligible slurring mumble, Theresa was thankful when Mary spoke to the nurse, and the woman moved to another room.

Aware of yet another stroke, plus the diagnosis of pneumonia, Theresa's physical comfort came from Mary rubbing and scratching her feet. Why did they itch so badly? How long had she been in the hospital this time? Wanting desperately to go home to her own bed, she understood the seriousness of her situation but wasn't afraid. Her family was beginning to gather.

She still had things to say. When not dozing, she'd reach for a pen while Mary or Jeff or someone else in the room held a pad for her. Why couldn't she write more clearly? She kept scrawling on the paper, attempting words that came out incoherent, and listening to everyone guess at what she wanted to communicate. A frustrating and impossible game of Pictionary.

Light streamed through the window. It must be daytime, again.

Mary brushed back Theresa's hair. "Mom. I called Melissa. She's flying in tomorrow."

Theresa clutched Mary's hand.

Time possessed no normalcy, and she slept. Theresa recognized the friends and family coming to visit. Yet, she abandoned trying to respond and just maintained eye contact with them. Perhaps God stifled her ability to speak so she might listen. And so she listened. Some expressed thanks for her being there for them through the rough patches. Others shared how much they loved her and would never forget her. A few could only express themselves through tears and hugs. Theresa worried about many of them. How would they get along?

Melissa entered the room as Mary sat holding Theresa's hand and Jeff stood at the foot of the bed.

"Hey, Mom," Melissa whispered as she took ahold of Theresa's other hand.

Theresa cherished the warmth of each of her daughter's touch. She squeezed their hands and looked at her children. The three beautiful human beings she birthed into the world. She motioned for her pen and paper and did her best to draw a heart to represent her love of family. Something she hoped to leave them with.

Mary looked at Melissa and said in a broken voice, "She's been waiting for you to come. Until we were all together."

Opening her eyes, Theresa still held no gauge of time, but the dark meant it was night, again. Melissa sat alone, next to her bed.

Her daughter rose and came close. She smiled and stroked Theresa's head. "I love you, Mom."

Reaching for the pad, Theresa penned a sloppy but legible, 'I (heart) you.'

Melissa leaned over the bed. "I want to share our adoption story in a book. Is that alright?"

She and Melissa spoke over the years about telling their story. Now, it would happen. Theresa scribbled on the paper the word, 'Write.'

When she opened her eyes the next time, Theresa finally saw her and felt Melissa helping to lift her arm. She reached her hand towards the one waiting for her. Her Momma. Oh, how she missed her. Soon, she would be home once more. Home again with Momma. She had so, so much to tell her.

AFTERWORD BY THE AUTHOR

Theresa was my biological mother. I am switching now to use the real name most knew her by, Terri.

For those wanting to read a bit more about the actual story, I have included some additional items. But, please read the book *first*, don't start here as there will be spoilers.

Terri (Theresa)

Terri possessed an immense compassion for people. It didn't matter if you were bloods, steps, halves, exes, in-laws, adopted, or anything else. She worried about and tried to help them all. That's who she was. Considering everyone as family, she always had room in her heart for one more. Thus prompting the title of the book - *Room For Another*.

For those who know me, they're aware I'm also an independent filmmaker. When asked how I got into film, I mention a personal experience that inspired me to write my first feature-length screenplay. This adoption story was it, albeit modified and much shorter.

Terri was a gifted storyteller and one I can only hope to emulate. She spent many years as a teacher and writer for a newspaper. We often talked about writing a book together—one of those procrastinated projects. On her deathbed, she enthusiastically encouraged me to write our story.

Charlie (Edward) and Millie (Catherine)

I am immensely thankful that God and Terri chose Charlie and Millie as my adoptive parents. Without them, who knows what direction my life would have taken.

My best friend, Karen, who I've known since we were three years old, because of our dads working together, said her siblings always considered me to be spoiled because my mom fixed my hair in long ringlets and sewed all my clothes when I was a little girl. My dad was always able to be coerced into something I wanted and frequently crooned to me *Home on the Range* (especially the chorus), *Wild Blue Yonder* (my father was a marine), or *I've Been Working on the Railroad* (Dinah was his nickname for me and "Dinah, won't you blow" was in the lyrics). He never could carry a tune!

My mom became a full-time, dedicated mother once they adopted my brother, Kenny (Robby) from the orphanage. She was a talented artist creating many beautiful items. My father was employed by the same company his whole working life. He took a promotion, moving us to England for my six years of elementary school. During that time, we traveled throughout Europe and went to Africa affording me such an opportunity to witness multiple cultures and appreciate what we have in the United States.

In 1995, my parents celebrated their fiftieth wedding anniversary. I wrote the following story, framed it, and presented it to them as my gift. It was a testament of their love for each other and for me.

The Old Woman

Yesterday, I met an old woman sitting alone by the lake. We struck up a casual conversation. She then became very serious and asked if she could share something with me. Of course, I obliged and listened intently as the old woman started telling me about two wonderful and loving individuals who evidently had a major impact on her life.

She laughed as she recalled how as a child, she believed her parents had found her in the ditch. That they had brought her home, washed her off, and decided to keep her. I watched her face light up as she spoke of how loving her mother and father had been throughout her life.

Through wrinkled skin, she smiled, as the simple memories of childhood played in her mind. The woman recounted that her parents were never selfish, they always gave more than their share, and how they had remained supportive of her through many trying times in her life.

While shifting her frail body, the woman described that as she grows older she can see how much of an influence these two beautiful people had on her life. They were great role models for teaching about working hard, supporting those you love, and the importance of responsibility. She learned about appreciating what you have while always striving to better oneself.

Tears filled the old woman's eyes as she told me of her children who were grown and had families of their own. And how her parents had loved them as they had loved her—openly and unconditionally.

The woman then grew quiet. She stared at the lake and all the beauty surrounding it. She was remembering—remembering her life and the people she loved. After a long time had passed, she looked back at me. At almost a whisper the old woman said, "I will be with them again one day, you know."

And I believed her.

To the most special parents in the world on your 50th Wedding Anniversary. Thanks for picking me up out of the ditch!

Love, Diane
(December 6, 1995)

Alright, perhaps I was spoiled, but I certainly didn't act selfish or privileged. My parents taught me about gratefulness and humility. We were a typical middle-class family. The things they purchased were always modest, well cared for, and kept forever. It took me almost a year to go through their home after they passed in 2008, just nine months apart. What I'd give to once again sit out on my mom and dad's back patio for hours just talking about anything and everything. They were wonderful, gracious, and loving people.

I remember my dad telling me the ditch and nursery stories mentioned in the book. It made me feel special. I know now that I was.

Tommy (Tony)

Despite the delay in meeting my biological father, Tommy, it did eventually happen. I recall the crazy day when I walked on that putting green at the car dealership, taking a huge chance of rejection. But when he held my hand in his, he communicated something very important. Regardless of the circumstances surrounding how I came into being during that single, fateful evening during college, he accepted responsibility and wanted to meet me. I am grateful for our ongoing relationship and his continued love.

Terri Meets My Parents

One of my favorite memories occurred the day Terri finally met Millie and Charlie for the first and only time. To be honest, I can't remember exactly what conversation took place. You'd think I would remember every last detail, but I suppose it simply became an overload of emotions. To think about the amount of love in that room just because of me was overwhelming.

In the book, Terri left a note for Millie in the bathroom. Actually, those true sentiments came delivered in a letter written to me from Terri with instructions to allow Millie to read them.

Terri's Passing

I cherished sitting alongside Terri in her last days on this earth. It held both heart-wrenching and heart-warming moments as I encountered people with whom she had a profound impact. Later, strangers reached out to tell me of their respect for

Terri and how she had touched their lives. They all knew about me—the baby she had given up for adoption.

In the end, Terri seemed happy to be surrounded by family, us expressing our love, stroking her hair, rubbing her feet, and holding her hands through her final transition. She was a strong woman who tried to communicate with us until just an hour before she died. Terri fought literally until her very last breath, and as you now know, her life was not easy.

My half-sister, Lora (Mary) helped Terri through numerous health issues. They remained best friends and shared an unbreakable mother-daughter bond. Many understand the difficulty of losing a parent. Whether blood-related or not, it's one of the hardest things to deal with, especially if you're close to them.

Although her departure from this life hurts the hearts of many, Terri is now free of pain and reunited with ones gone before. Maybe she is even hanging out with Charlie and Millie, my Uncle Bill (Phil), and Nancy (Jackie). But definitely with her Momma. May God bless and comfort all of us who have loved and lost.

Diane's Blog Post on May 30, 2018 (www.dianedresback.com)

My Two Mothers

Motherhood can come in many shapes and forms and can last for varying periods of time. It often means doing what's best for the child regardless of the pain for the adult.

Terri (1936-2016) and Millie (1921-2008) did not share the same generation. They were born over 2,600 miles apart. As children, they experienced contrasting family dynamics and backgrounds. Their formal education and work histories did not overlap. By all accounts, these women lived far and away vastly different lives from each other.

Yet, they both shared a belief in the opportunity of adoption. Ultimately, the sacrifice of one became the blessing of the other. A decision based solely and mutually in love.

I retain an immense respect for adopting parents who provide for the emotional and physical needs of a child (of any age). Those who welcome children openly into a new life of acceptance and belonging.

My humble appreciation also goes to those women who decide to carry a baby and selflessly embrace adoption as a way to fulfill the family desires of others.

Most of us have been touched by adoption in some way or another. If not firsthand, surely through someone we know. Every situation is as unique as the circumstances and individuals involved.

Perhaps children receive the chance to meet their biological parents. Not all situations turn out positive for there are no guarantees. But, sometimes they work out better than imagined.

I was blessed with long relationships with both these wonderful, beautiful, and strong women—my two mothers. And I am extremely thankful for their decisions and actions.

Terri and Millie contributed to who I am now. I wish I could call and talk with them. Alas, both have moved on from this life. Yet my many memories and profound gratitude to each, will never cease.

I love you—my two mothers!

View Actual Photographs

I thought it would be fun after readers have finished *Room For Another*, to see some actual photographs of the characters in the book. These pictures are on my author website under a special link.

Simply visit www.dianedresback.com. Under the Books tab, pick *Room For Another*. On the page near the bottom, you will see the word PHOTOS. Please note, reading the book *first* is highly recommended otherwise there will be some spoilers.

Terri's Poetry

"I have written poetry for years—just as my expression to myself of my emotions. I found, as a child, that these emotions need to be vented and if there is no one to listen or the feelings are too deep to be shared, write them and you feel better."

Terri Cox (February 1981)

Untitled #1 (1959)

The rain on the roof
Is music to my ears
for now I can cry
And hide all my tears.

Run and stand on the porch.
Lift my face to the sky.
Simply let go -
And have a good cry.

When my tears are all gone,
And the sobbing is through,
Tomorrow will be better
For I'll start out all new.

The bad feelings are gone,
And good ones will replace.
Tomorrow, I'll go around
With a smile on my face.

Untitled #2 (1959)

Love is the mother-image of the world.
She has the power of construction and destruction.

Her outreaching fingers are curled around the heart
to hold fast so that her work cannot be undone.

Original First Letters

Below are the first letters between mother and daughter. Everything is verbatim except for using the fictitious names used in the book to keep things clear. Theresa (Terri) was 44 and Melissa (Diane) was 21 years old (forgive my grammatical errors and awkward phrasing, haha!).

Note that some of the details are slightly different than those presented in the book. Terri shared her stories with me several times and those particulars fluctuated a bit. You know how it is when you remember things from long ago? Sometimes the story changes slightly.

December 29, 1980

Dear Melodie,

I was told many years ago that was your name, but I'm still not too sure. I called you 'Jackie' when you were born and in my mind for the last twenty-one years.

A letter of this kind is exceedingly hard to write. Words don't seem to fall into place easily. My mind is a mud-puddle of what questions you may want answered and still I'm not quite sure of what you really want. I hope that we can get together, if this is your wish, and talk sometime in the near future. But, until then, I must proceed with what is uppermost in my thoughts and heart concerning your birth.

I have known and talked with many adopted children in my teaching career and their uppermost concern seems to be that of "not being wanted" and therefore "being given away." Realistically, this does happen sometimes. In our situation this couldn't have been farther from the truth. Thus begins our story.

When I found, at first, that I was pregnant, I didn't want to be that way and considered illegal (it was then) abortion as a way out. It was not the law or money factor that stopped me, but love for the tiny life inside my body. My next emotion was fear of other people's thoughts and their condemning me as a "bad girl." I considered suicide and again the love of you stirring inside stopped me. I had only two choices.

One of my choices was to keep you and to try and cope with society and its possible cruelness to us both. But then, raising you without a father's love seemed as cruel to you as what people might say to either you or me. A child needs both parents to love and raise him/her to have the best possible foundation for life. I could not provide both and therefore I could not provide the stability I wanted you to have.

The other alternative was adoption. First, I visited two maternity homes in Los Angeles. I interviewed with both and found them to be professionally understanding but cold inside. My requests to them were—I must see my baby, hold it, and know that it was physically okay. The other was that I know, as positively as possible, that the adoptive parents would love, first, and provide, second, for my baby. The agencies would not even consider either request.

It was at this time that a mutual friend of your adoptive father's and mine that put me in touch with a lawyer that could and would handle adoptions. These type of adoptions were known as Grey Market. They were risky to adoptive parents in that the birth mother could take the child back up to a certain time limit. I believe it was around six months, or so. I can understand how frightened your adoptive parents must have felt during my pregnancy and your first year of life. What they did not know about me was I had carefully considered and made up my mind. Only one thing could have changed it and I had determined that, too. If you had been born physically disabled in any way, I would have raised you—my thought being, at that time, that a disabled child could only be loved best by its real mother. Looking back now, how immature I was.

It was arranged, by the lawyer, for me to live with your Dear Uncle Phil. I dropped out of college just prior to my last semester, senior year, and moved in with him. I'm sorry you could not have known Phil in your adult life. He was a warm, understanding, kind man, and he loved you long before you were born. I can remember only one time did he try to change my mind about your being given up. Phil loved me and cared for me as a father would have his child. I thank God he was there. Just before you were born, Phil took me to a jewelry store to purchase a small gold cross for you. I don't know if you have it or what happened to it, but it was to be a sign to you that both God and I loved you.

When you were born, I watched and held you. You were brought to me later for feeding and I checked you more thoroughly than any doctor could have. I know now that I was endeavoring to find any defect. There was not one. I removed an extra diaper that they had wrapped around your bottom and hid it under my pillow. I kissed you and then called the nurse to take you. My best friend, Jackie, came and got me.

Giving you up was truly the hardest thing I have ever done in my life. I still have your newborn picture and your diaper tucked safely away. I can't tell you how many times over the years I have touched both and thought about you. For a long time I kept track of you and your parents through Phil, until he passed away, and later through a mutual friend. Only when I was convinced that you were taken care of and loved, did I stop checking on you.

The above will not answer a lot of your questions, I'm sure. It may only raise more. It is a starting place. If you wish to know more or know me and my family as we are now, I don't know. I will tell you that you have a half brother, seventeen, and a half sister, sixteen, that are aware you are out there somewhere. I am now an ancient forty-four years!

I will stop this "lengthy" story amid old tears with this thought for you. Your parents, for that is what they truly are, have my deepest appreciation for your loving upbringing. They have given to you what too many children never have had—a home, guidance, and steady loving hands. A mother or father is not made by the fact of birth alone. A mother and father are "grown" over the years of raising and caring for a child. I did not interfere and I will not interfere with your love of them or theirs for you. I do know, however, that there is room in all of us for adding another love. Accept mine, as it has always been there even though you were not aware of it.

You are free to write me or call if you would like. I would like to know you.

With Love, your other mother, Theresa

January 15, 1981

Dear Theresa,

It's kind of strange to start this way, but I don't really know what I'm supposed to call you! I understand your difficulty now in writing a letter like this, I'm feeling the same way.

I guess I should tell you right away and hope to reassure you that I never thought I was unwanted. My parents never kept the fact from me that I was adopted, and I appreciate that. It seems like I've always known and have been very open about it. When my friends and I get on the subject, I feel no embarrassment to admit that I was adopted. They ask me if it bothers me, and I look them straight in the eye and say, "not in the slightest way." I explain to them that I have the greatest respect for Theresa (as I was told your name was), and that the strength and courage you showed by giving me up, proved you were an exceptional person, and one with an extremely unselfish love.

But, even though my home life has always been happy, my feeling for my 'unknown' natural mother was one of great curiosity. The biggest part, I guess, was and still is (for a while longer) what you look like. I was told by a very dear old man that I looked like you. If I looked into a mirror I would see your face.

That dear old man is my Uncle Phil. Theresa, he has not passed away, thank God. He is alive and living in Oregon. Once a year I see him when he comes to visit his step daughter. He never forgets my birthday or any other occasion. And he speaks very highly of you. You were very special to him. He is by far my favorite uncle. He always has been and now I understand why I was his favorite niece. I was a part of you.

Last February (1980) when I saw him, we got on the subject of you. I hadn't know much before, but he revealed a lot for me. Eagerly, I asked if he knew how to get in touch with you. Unfortunately, all he knew was that you were up north somewhere.

My Uncle Phil had given me new hope in the search of my natural mother. I talked with a few of my close friends and we tried to figure out ways to find you. There was only one thing holding us back, we knew you had married, and we didn't know your married name. The months went on and one day my father received a call from Ben (I believe that was his name). This happened right out of the blue, no warning. I knew right then and there, that my curiosity would soon be ended. Except for one very real possibility.

Last year in school, I took a speech class. One of the speeches I selected was on adopted children. In short, I said I felt that after the child reaches a certain age, they should (if they care to) have the right to know someone of their own 'flesh and blood.' I suggested there be some type of intermediary organization to help contact the other party. But, I strongly made the point that these so called 'middle-people' would contact the other party first to ensure that it was safe and emotionally acceptable to bring the two people back together. If not, then it should not be done.

I feel I've been very fortunate not only that you wanted to contact me, but because you have thought of me through the years.

My parents have brought me up very well (I feel). I believe I'm pretty emotionally stable and open minded. And, I have no doubt in my mind that we could become great friends and share a very special love.

I'll have to say, that when I got your letter, it was a good thing I was alone. I sat and looked at it for a long time. And, as I read it...I cried. Not an unhappy cry, mind you, but an overjoyed sob. I had answered a great question in my mind. I had found my natural mother.

I will give you my address here so you can send to my house instead of my Dad's. Oh, by the way, Melodie was close to my middle name.

But, I would like you to know that if you want to call me 'Jackie,' it wouldn't bother me a bit.

The photo's enclosed are 1) the most recent one of my family on my twenty-first birthday. 2) This is an older one. It was taken at my Senior Prom at High School (May 1977). I look approximately the same except for my hair is much longer now, and unfortunately I have acquired a few extra pounds!

I guess I will close now, but not in lack of things to tell you! I've so much to tell you about my last twenty-one years, and I've so much to ask you of yours. My mom had the gold cross and gave it back to me. It seems more beautiful to me now than ever before.

Take care and I hope this is just a beginning of what is to come.

Love, Melissa (alias Jackie)

Thank you for embarking on the journey within the pages of *Room For Another*. Your time and dedication to this story mean the world to me.

If you found inspiration and insight or enjoyed the book, I would be deeply grateful if you could take a moment to share your thoughts with others. Your review and/or rating can make a significant impact and is a testament to the power of storytelling.

Please consider leaving an honest review on platforms like Amazon, Goodreads, BookBub, or wherever you acquired your copy of the book. Your feedback, no matter how brief, is immensely valuable and much appreciated as it helps people discover meaningful stories.

Thanks again for being a part of this literary adventure. I'm excited to hear your reactions to *Room For Another*.

I would be honored to have you in my readers email group which allows me to let you know when I have news or new books and importantly giveaways and discounts. You can sign up at my website: www.dianedresback.com

Warm regards,
Diane

ABOUT THE AUTHOR

Diane has long been a lover of storytelling. She began her path down the world of sharing her stories in novels upon an unexpected move from Phoenix to Texas for 6 years. Now settled back in Phoenix, she continues to write. Diane also is passionate about independent filmmaking which offers her the opportunity to share her stories on film as well. She has written, directed, and/or produced a feature film and several short films winning numerous awards for her efforts including receiving the 2012 Arizona Filmmaker of the Year Award.

Diane spent 27 years in corporate Human Resources and Training primarily in management and executive-level positions in the financial and travel industries. She holds a Master's degree in Adult Education and a Bachelor's degree in Human Services.

Author & Blog Website: www.dianedresback.com

Filmmaking Website: www.mindclover.com

Facebook: https://www.facebook.com/dianedresback.author

Instagram: https://www.instagram.com/dianem.dresback/

Goodreads: https://www.goodreads.com/author/list/14179568.Diane_M_Dresback

BookBub: https://www.bookbub.com/authors/diane-dresback

BOOKS BY DIANE M. DRESBACK

TRILOGY

Awake As A Stranger trilogy
...*Awakening* (Book 1)
...*Rebellion* (Book 2)
...*Altercation* (Book 3)
Treaz and Omani reside on two different continents yet each are trapped in deplorable realities—Treaz living within other people's bodies and Omani being held captive on her uncle's compound. Both long to regain control over their lives, escape their merciless captors, and expose the haunting truths facing them and the world. Can they find freedom together?

STAND ALONES

Postponement
Technology allows for the delay of parenthood by cryo-suspension of newborns. Nora Collins navigates an ethical minefield and risks everything for one infant.

Reminisce
If your memories make you who you are, then what happens when you change them? Nick discovers a world of drug-induced memory manipulation in order to overcome his struggles.

Promise of Protection
What if YOU held the power to manipulate the well-being or the demise of many? Joe is called to a senior living facility 16 hours away. He unwillingly becomes entangled in unraveling the bizarre scientific work of his estranged father.

Room For Another: A Courageous Adoption Story Based on True Events
Every choice carries a consequence. After the death of her mother, an unloving stepmother, and an uninvolved father, Theresa must deal with another trauma—an unwanted pregnancy.

NONFICTION

From Us For You: Inspiring Stories of Healing, Growth and Transformation
25 inspiring stories of healing, growth and transformation compiled from women and meant to encourage and inspire readers. Net-profits of book sales are donated to a nonprofit advocating for and assisting in the needs of women.

Your Action, Your Success: Motivating Yourself To Get Things Done
What stops you from getting more done? Fear? Time? Procrastination? This book offers easy, no-nonsense tips and strategies to help yourself get more things accomplished.

To find out more or purchase any of these books, please visit www.dianedresback.com

Printed in Dunstable, United Kingdom